"The perfect blend of theory and step ___ ___ n you
thought there was nothing left to say ___ ___ s
Sandy Frank's *Inner Game of Screenwr.*

—LAWRENCE KONNER, writer ___ ___ *...os*, screenwriter: *The
Jewel of the Nile, Planet of the Apes, Superman IV: The Quest for
Peace, Star Trek VI: The Undiscovered Country*

"*The Inner Game of Screenwriting* offers the kind of wisdom writers can
understand. Not only does Sandy cast a sharp eye on the emotional
aspects of screenplay construction, but he understands what a script really
needs in order to be commercial. Invaluable."

—JOEL SURNOW, creator: *24*

"In my job, I read a lot of scripts—good, bad, and all things in between. I
can honestly say, if you read and heed this book, you will be ahead of the
game. Written with tremendous insight and a candor that is rare, Sandy
provides practical advice that will benefit the inexperienced or experienced
writer. I highly recommend it!"

—DAVID STAPF, President, CBS Television Studios

"Sandy Frank understands and explains screenplay structure better than
any other writer I've worked with. His advice has always improved my
scripts."

—LAWRENCE O'DONNELL, Emmy-winning executive producer
and writer of *The West Wing*, host of *The Last Word with
Lawrence O'Donnell* (MSNBC)

"Sandy Frank's *The Inner Game of Screenwriting* starts by explaining that the writing of scripts can be divided into two components—the inner (emotional/character-driven), and outer (plot-driven) games. The premise is that for a film or show to be successful, the inner game must be solid. The interesting thing is, in the book's seven parts, the theory is explained, tested, and even challenged by the author, using generous examples. This is a thorough look at why some films/TV shows (including adaptations, sequels, and remakes), resonate stronger with audiences than others, and how to write these kinds of scripts yourself."

—Erin Corrado, OneMovieFiveReviews.com

20 WINNING STORY FORMS

THE INNER GAME OF *Screenwriting*

SANDY FRANK

MICHAEL WIESE PRODUCTIONS

Published by Michael Wiese Productions
12400 Ventura Blvd. #1111
Studio City, CA 91604
(818) 379-8799, (818) 986-3408 (FAX)
mw@mwp.com
www.mwp.com

Cover design by Johnny Ink. www.johnnyink.com
Interior design by Jay Anning
Printed by McNaughton & Gunn

Manufactured in the United States of America

Library of Congress Cataloging-in-Publication Data

Frank, Sandy, 1954–
  The inner game of screenwriting : 20 winning story forms / Sandy Frank.
    p. cm.
  ISBN 978-1-61593-061-6
  1. Motion picture authorship. 2. Television authorship. I. Title.
  PN1996.F73 2011
  808.2'3–dc23
                              2011017958

To my perfect Pam,
who loved and supported me
every step of the way

CONTENTS

Part One
INTRODUCING THE INNER GAME OF SCREENWRITING

This book will introduce the concept of the **Inner Game of Screenwriting**. It's a "big picture" theory, describing not the hundred things your screenplay needs, but the single biggest thing a screenplay needs to be successful—an Inner Game. It's strategy, not tactics.

This first part of the book will describe the Inner Game of Screenwriting in detail.

CHAPTER ONE

THE INNER GAME OF SCREENWRITING

HOW CAN YOU USE THIS BOOK? If you're a screenwriter—novice or pro—you probably picked this book up because you'd like to learn more about writing a screenplay. But why is that? If you're like most screenwriters, you've taken courses and read books on the subject. You may even have gone to college to study it.

So why don't you already know how to do it? Why is screenwriting so hard?

Let's start off with a metaphor. A guy who knows absolutely nothing about golf, has never played it or even seen it, hears that it's a fun game and decides he wants to play. So he goes to a local golf coach and asks for lessons.

The coach is happy to take him on. He tells him that he has boiled the game down to the essentials. Lessons like "Keep your head down" and "Keep your left elbow straight."

The new student dives right in and works and practices harder than anyone ever has. His drives at the range get longer and straighter and his putting gets more accurate. He just keeps getting better and better.

Finally, he goes out on his own to play his first game, and shoots a 160. (If you're unfamiliar with golf, that's really, really bad.)

Why did he do so badly? Not because of anything the coach told him, but because of something the coach *didn't* tell him — that the object of the game is to get the ball into the holes in the fewest number of strokes.

Now that may seem silly, because everyone knows that. But if you think about it, there could be other objectives — to hit the ball as *high* as possible, or to use the clubs in numerical order. Or think about a game you're unfamiliar with, maybe the Japanese game of Go. It's not inconceivable that you could take Go lessons for a while, learning how to make moves, but without learning how you win the game. The point is that the hypothetical golf student never learned his *objective*, what he was ultimately trying to accomplish.

I sometimes feel that the same is true for us screenwriters — we've never been taught exactly what it is we're trying to do. So we write and we write, and sometimes it works out and sometimes it doesn't, but we often don't know why.

Ask screenwriters what they're trying to do when they sit down to start their screenplays, and what kinds of answers would you expect? Some, especially if they're getting paid, will say that they're trying to fill 110 pages with properly formatted description and dialog. I remember years ago, a friend of mine — he wasn't a screenwriter, he was a bond trader — told me that he had just written a screenplay. At the time I was a television writer thinking about tackling a spec feature, so I asked him how he went about it. His bemused answer: he started typing on page one and stopped when he reached 110. Not exactly the advice I was looking for.

Others might tell you they're trying to tell a good story, but that just changes the question to "What's a good feature story?" After all, there are plenty of amusing stories I've heard at dinner that wouldn't make good features. There are plenty of gripping news stories that wouldn't, either.

There's a lot of information about screenwriting out there, and we all learn things like: keep the dialog snappy, start scenes late, hit your act breaks around pages 30 and 90. But few authors or teachers explain to us our *ultimate goal*: what, in simple terms, are we trying to do?

Not because they're trying to keep it a secret, but because they don't know either. After all, if somebody knew—really *knew*— what made a screenplay good, wouldn't word get around and then wouldn't every screenplay be pretty good? Instead, even the "best" screenplays, the ones that actually get bought and shot on film and shown in theaters, are still hit-or-miss. Even a screenwriter who writes one great screenplay can go on to fail at his next. So there's something that remains mysterious about the process.

The challenge is to figure out what a screenplay needs without being too reductive, too simplistic. After all, it would be pretty silly to say, here are the ten things your screenplay needs, and if you put them all in, the screenplay will be a hit. Are there ten sure steps to writing a best-selling novel or painting a great painting? Of course not. But I do think there's something a screenplay needs to be successful. What is it?

I call it the **Inner Game**.

To switch metaphors (sorry, writing about writing involves a lot of them), if you were looking to build a house, you'd hire at least two people with very different jobs. You'd get an architect, whose job would be to come up with the overall design. He would draw you a picture of what the finished product would look like — a one-story Spanish or a two-story Alpine. Then he'd draw a blueprint of the building. He'd be in charge of the overall idea of the house.

When you were satisfied with the overall plan you'd hire another guy, a builder. A guy who knew how to make the foundation sturdy, the corners square, and the windows pretty. He'd take the architect's blueprint and implement it in the real world.

The thing to notice is how different these two guys' skill sets are. If the architect were required to build the house he designed, you might very well end up with a beautiful but poorly-built house. One with a cool shape but whose windows stuck and whose wood was the wrong thickness.

Contrariwise, if the builder had to design the house from scratch, you could end up with a house with beautifully hung doors and perfect stucco, but with the windows all on the back and no light in the bedrooms. If you walked around the house and inspected it from one foot away, it would look great. But if you were ten or twenty feet away, you'd see it was a mess.

That's why we hire two different guys — an architect and a builder. But, as screenwriters, we have to do *both* jobs.

First, the screenplay architecture; the formation of the overall story and shape of the screenplay. Then the building: crafting

the scenes and dialog. Again, these are very different skill sets—
some of us are great at one, but not so good at the other. I've met
screenwriters who could come up with an amazing story, but
unfortunately produced lax scenes and leaden dialog. And I've met
others who could come up with tight scenes and sparkling dialog,
but in service to a story you couldn't care less about.

With a house, the building is important because you may be
living there for years. But with a movie, we're not going to live in
it; we're just going to walk through. So while both of these aspects
are important to screenwriting, the overall architecture is by far
the more important.

This book is about architecture, not building. It's "big picture."
It's not the fox, who knows many little things; it's the hedgehog,
who knows one big thing. In surveying bookstores and Amazon
for screenwriting books, I found that the largest category by far is
the builder category (to continue my metaphor), containing books
with titles along the lines of *112 Ways to Make Your Screenplay
Sizzle*. And plenty of books specifically focusing on crafting scenes
or writing dialog.

There are also lots of books that tell you where to put the
act breaks and other points your screenplay has to hit. This
sort of book started back with the introduction of the three-act
structure with its two act breaks, later adding midpoints, etc.
Plenty of books exist today to give screenwriters the three, five,
or fifteen scenes they have to have on certain pages to make their
screenplays successful.

Both of these book categories are helpful. I have read them
and learned useful things from them. It is, after all, important to
be able to write good dialog and to use reasonable proportions

in your screenplay. But my impression on assessing the market is that the architect books are quite rare. Yet, to me, they're the most important.

So what do we need to write a good screenplay?

Let's go back to the sports analogy: every screenplay has two aspects, which I'll call the Inner Game and the Outer Game.

The **Outer Game** is what we usually think of as the plot. It's what's going on onscreen, out in the world. Take as an example the fine movie *The Queen*: the Outer Game is how Queen Elizabeth II deals with the tragic death of Princess Diana.

The queen starts out wanting the royal family to say, essentially, nothing about the accident. She's not much for displays of emotion, and tries to get by with a simple statement of regret. But her Prime Minister realizes that this won't do in twentieth century England and urges the queen to give her grief-stricken subjects more. Finally, to avoid damage to the monarchy, she does exactly that.

All in all, a reasonably interesting story, aided by the brilliant acting of Helen Mirren as Elizabeth.

But that's not why the audiences loved it. What really drove the success of the movie was its finely wrought Inner Game—what's going on *inside* Her Majesty.

Elizabeth starts the movie as somewhat cold, seemingly unable to convey emotion or form strong personal relationships. But over the course of the movie she changes. She starts to see that the personal touch is important for a monarch and ends up transforming from cool and withdrawn to warmer and more demonstrative. And not as a cynical ploy: it's a genuine change. A satisfying Inner Game, and the audience sparked to it.

Which brings me to the Inner Game of Screenwriting principle:

■ **A relentless focus on the Inner Game is the key to writing a successful screenplay.**

WHY THE INNER GAME?

Which may cause you to ask—why would this be what audiences are after? Why would we want to see someone change? Why should this be more satisfying than car chases or political intrigue?

Because we like to watch other people go through what we go through. Not literally, of course. After all, none of us will ever issue a royal statement about Princess Diana's car crash. But even if the problems confronting movie characters aren't our problems, we can still relate to them because they can still *symbolize* our problems.

All of us human beings have flaws and try to overcome them. We watch movies to see other characters struggle with that same ordeal. Even if the problems are different, the process is the same.

Consider *Liar Liar*. Jim Carrey's character, Fletcher Reede, is a pathologically lying lawyer who has to learn to live an honest life. Now, 99% of us already know that habitual lying is morally wrong and a bad life strategy. We realized it long ago and don't need to overcome that particular problem.

But we have our own problems. Maybe we're selfish, or cowardly, or overbearing. Unless we're perfect, we've got shortcomings, and if we're good people, we try to overcome them. Sometimes we succeed, sometimes we fail, and it can be a difficult, even frightening process. So when we watch Reede wrestle with his lying, we empathize because of our own failings, our own struggles.

We like to watch others go through the same ordeal we go through, and we cheer when they succeed. It reminds us of our own triumphs and goads us to revisit our failures. For most of us, that's what life is ultimately about.

Not that a screenplay's Outer Game is completely unimportant. But it's important in a particular way: the Outer Game provides the opportunity for the main character to go through the Inner Game. And, of course, opportunity for the audience to watch it and the studio to market it.

Matching Inner and Outer Games can be tricky. It would be obscene to suggest that—in the real world—the Holocaust took place so Oskar Schindler could become a better person. But in the context of the movie *Schindler's List*, that's exactly what happens.

This means that the writer has to be careful when pairing an Inner Game with an Outer. It would probably be a mistake to write a romantic comedy set in the Holocaust where the main character has to learn to be nicer to women. Or a movie set in Manhattan on 9/11 in which a taxi driver has to learn not to cheat his riders.

But the main point stands: the Outer Game is simply the excuse for the Inner Game. It's reminiscent of Hitchcock's theory of the MacGuffin.

To Hitchcock, the MacGuffin was a plot device that motivated the characters, but whose exact explanation was unimportant. The characters simply agree that the MacGuffin is important. A classic example is the "letters of transit" in *Casablanca*. If you think about them, they make no sense, but they serve as the thing that everyone in the movie is trying to get.

In the Inner Game theory, the entire Outer Game is, in a sense, a MacGuffin. What really matters is the Inner Game, what the main character goes through internally and how he changes. It doesn't really matter whether the main character goes through that change because he wants to win the big bowling tournament, or because his wife has gone missing. Either way, it's the Inner Game that counts.

Again, it's not that the Outer Game doesn't matter at all, but it's safe to say that while a movie with a strong Inner Game can work without much of an Outer Game, the reverse will be considerably more difficult. The problem with a lot of screenwriting instruction is that it concentrates so heavily on the Outer Game, stressing questions like, what is the main character trying to achieve, who is the opponent keeping him from achieving it, etc.

Let's look at an example of a movie with a strong Inner Game and not much of a conventional Outer Game: *Juno*, winner of the Oscar for Best Original Screenplay.

Juno—about a teenage girl who accidentally gets pregnant and decides to have the baby and give it up for adoption—is missing many of the conventional Outer Game elements. Is there an opponent (touted as absolutely necessary by many screenwriting teachers) who makes Juno's quest progressively more difficult to accomplish? No. Is there plot twist after plot twist making Juno's quest harder and harder as the movie goes on? Uh, no. The truth is, Juno has her baby and gives it up without much opposition. Not a single character in the movie tells her "You can't do that."

But let's imagine a writer who's been conventionally trained to come up with an elaborate Outer Game trying to flesh out a screenplay about a pregnant teenager who wants to give up her baby for adoption. We'll call the resulting movie *Bizarro Juno*.

First, according to conventional wisdom, the girl would need a powerful opponent. Someone to oppose her in her desire to give her baby up for adoption to a couple she's chosen.

How about the head of the local Children's Services Department, someone with the right to say *yes* or *no* to the teen's choice for adoptive parents? Now let's throw in some problems and reversals—let's say the couple Bizarro Juno chooses to adopt her baby doesn't make enough money to satisfy the Children's Services bureaucrat, so she has to arrange for them to pretend to live in a nicer house than their real one. But mere minutes before the final interview, the real owner unexpectedly comes home and comedy ensues….

Would *Bizzaro Juno* be a good movie? I suppose it's possible, but I think it's safe to say it wouldn't be winning any writing awards. Yet that is the sort of concentration on the Outer Game that most screenplay instruction insists on.

So why, without that sort of elaborate Outer Game, does the actual *Juno* succeed so well? Not surprisingly, it's all about the Inner Game.

At the beginning of the movie, Juno MacGuff (Ellen Page) is funny, but she's also cynical and off-putting, carefully keeping the people in her life at a distance. Her relationship with her dad is okay, but not particularly deep; she doesn't much care for her stepmother, occasionally demonstrating this by puking in her front hallway vase; and even the boy who impregnates her she keeps at arm's length (at least figuratively), more a curiosity than a boyfriend.

But at the end of the movie, having made her way through the Outer Game, having had her baby and given it up for adoption, Juno stands transformed—she's closer to her dad; she's seen her stepmother, for the first time, as the strong, loving person she really is; and her relationship with her boyfriend has blossomed into love. She has truly grown from a standoff-ish cynic into a loving young woman. And this Inner Game is what the audience was reacting to by making the movie such a big hit.

None of this is to say, of course, that's there's anything wrong with having an opponent. But the opponent should be there for a purpose, not as an end in itself. The opponent's purpose is to help create the Outer Game, the difficulties that will push the main character through the Inner Game. If the opponent's not doing that, then you should reconsider what he's doing in the story, and if you have some other way to force the main character through the Inner Game, you may not even need an opponent.

So there you have it. Of course I don't pretend to have discovered Inner Game — screenwriting instruction has always included character arcs. But here's the main point — if the audience has to choose between a strong Inner Game and a strong Outer Game, they'll choose the Inner Game every time. After all, what would you prefer — a big Outer Game with car chases and explosions but with small characters you couldn't care less about, or a smaller, quieter Outer Game with characters you care deeply about, and who go through profound changes?

It's one of those 80/20 rules. If you get the Inner Game right, even if the page-by-page writing isn't that great, you'll end up with an okay movie. If you screw up on the Inner Game, even if the dialog is wonderful, you'll have a movie that doesn't work.

So, remember the Inner Game principle:

■ **A relentless focus on the Inner Game is the key to writing a successful screenplay.**

A final metaphor. When a psychotherapist listens to a patient describe a dream, he doesn't react to the literal "plot" of the dream; he strives to uncover the dream's hidden meaning. In fact, if your therapist listens to your dream and says "You say you cut off your mother's head, but that's not how a chainsaw works," you should probably look for a new therapist.

The audience is like a good therapist: it's listening to what happened in the dream, but it's looking for the underlying meaning. It's watching the movie's Outer Game, but it's reacting to its Inner Game. People, including critics, who concentrate on the Outer Game are, in fact, being ridiculously literal about movies, ignoring the symbolism embodied by the Inner Game. Missing the forest for the trees, they'll say things like "*The Hurt Locker* is the perfect war movie." It indicates to me that they don't have a clue what the movie is really about. Would they describe *Moby Dick* as the perfect whale movie?

Some reviews don't amount to much more than recounting the Outer Game and saying whether the writer liked the movie. Oblivious to the Inner Game and its symbolism, these reviews are about as silly as reviewing *Animal Farm* like it was about real animals.

And some critics actively dislike Inner Game. Take this comment from critic Jennie Yabroff from a *Newsweek* review of *Dinner for Schmucks*:

> The imperative of modern American comedies is that the
> protagonists change and grow, and that growth always takes
> place in the direction of societal norms … Though the premise
> of *Dinner for Schmucks* is deeply cruel, we are supposed to laugh,
> because we trust that by the closing credits the characters will

have matured into upstanding men. Too bad Hollywood doesn't give the audience credit for being mature, too.

A pretty clear indictment of Inner Game as a silly, immature thing holding movies back. The evidence seems clear, however, that audiences still overwhelmingly appreciate conventional Inner Games.

Once you realize what the audience is really looking for, you can concentrate your efforts on satisfying their expectations.

And by the way, if you're not a screenwriter, but just want to learn how screenplays and movies work, this book will explain it to you. You'll enjoy watching movies and analyzing them, and you'll enjoy sharing your theories about them at dinner parties.

◆ ◆ ◆

The rest of this book will flesh out the Inner Game of Screenwriting, introduce you to the different Inner Game Archetypes, and show you how to build them.

EXERCISE

Make a list of your five favorite movies. Then write down your favorite (remembered) scenes from them.

How many of those favorite scenes are big scenes in the Inner Games of the movies?

CHAPTER TWO

A SUCCESSFUL INNER GAME—*THE QUEEN*

T O REVISIT THE DIFFERENCE between the Inner and Outer Games, let's take another look at a recent movie with a successful Inner Game: *The Queen*—a small film that was both a critical and box-office hit, taking in more than $120 million worldwide on an estimated budget of about $15 million.

Let's look again at the film's Outer Game. *The Queen* is based on the real-life events surrounding the death of Princess Diana in her tragic auto accident. The focus is on Queen Elizabeth and her public reaction to the crash.

In Elizabeth's mind, Diana—divorced from Prince Charles— is no longer a member of the Royal Family, and is therefore not entitled to any response by them: no public statement, no flags flying at half-staff, and absolutely no royal funeral. But Diana's adoring public disagrees, and Prime Minister Tony Blair counsels the Queen to go along with their wishes. The Outer Game turns on this decision.

The Inner Game meshes closely with the Outer. The Inner Game is about Elizabeth's emotional state. The film's thesis is that the Queen, with her British stiff upper lip, is too uptight, not emotional enough. That's her personal flaw, and she has to overcome it by learning to let go and express her emotions openly.

The Outer Game, while kind of interesting, isn't going to fill U.S. theater seats. After all, are American viewers really going to care if the British monarchy survives the death of Diana? Or whether the Queen or the Prime Minister gains the upper hand?

But we *are* going to care about Elizabeth, the movie's main character, and whether she can overcome her psychological/emotional flaw, because it symbolizes to us our own inner struggles with our own flaws. It's this Inner Game that really drives the screenplay. We want to watch her grow from emotionally stunted to a fully emotional, fully involved human being.

That's the struggle we really invest in, and it's wonderfully developed in the script. Every scene fleshes out this theme: we see the Queen's relationships with not just the public, but with the Prime Minister, with her husband, her mother, her children, and her grandchildren. She's constantly confronted with versions of the choice she must ultimately make: to remain the same, unemotional woman, or to change, to become the emotionally involved person we hope she can be.

In the end, she makes the leap, makes the change. In the Outer Game, she allows a state funeral for Diana, and lets the royal family participate in various rituals in Diana's honor. But—to reiterate, yet again—the important thing is not the Outer Game, but the Inner. What the Queen does physically is important, but only insofar as it allows us to see what's going on inside. We get to see *why* she does these things.

She sees that her subjects loved Diana and that they need their Queen—no matter what her own personal opinion—to validate their feelings. If she cares for her subjects—and she does seem to—she needs to show that by celebrating Diana. Not as a cynical ploy to keep the royals in power, but genuinely and sincerely. That requires her to grow, to become a better person, and this she does. And this Inner Game satisfies the audience, who rewarded the movie with box office and praise.

Another way of putting the relationship between the Outer and Inner Games is this: the Outer Game is the skin and the Inner Game the skeleton of a screenplay. The audience sees the Outer Game, but it's the Inner Game that gives the screenplay the support it needs to stand and deliver its entertainment message.

To sum up, *The Queen* is a successful movie because of its well-developed Inner Game. The Outer Game—dealing with the death of Diana—is well done and it's what we see on the screen, but the absolutely crucial thing to realize and remember is that it merely provides the opportunity for Elizabeth to go through the Inner Game. That Inner Game—will the Queen become more emotionally open—is what really hits the audience in its collective heart.

And the audience responds even to that on a more abstract level. While the particular character flaw in this particular screenplay is lack of emotional openness, audiences respond to a main character's struggle to overcome *any* flaw. Her flaw may not be my flaw, but I've got plenty of my own.

Let me emphasize one more thing—I'm not saying that the Outer Game is completely unimportant. Audiences, of course, respond to well-crafted scenes and well-wrought dialog. This book's premise is not that a good Inner Game is *sufficient*, only that it's *necessary*.

The Queen is one of those exceptional movies that combine an involving Inner Game with a gripping Outer Game. It's a perfect example of what every screenwriter should aim for.

This book will explain how Inner Games work so you can make sure your screenplay has one, and that it's working correctly.

EXERCISE

Screen *The Queen*. Make a list of all the scenes that bear on the Inner Game of Elizabeth's emotional change, from cold and closed to warm and open. It's important to note that the most memorable scenes in the film are much more important to the Inner Game than they are to the Outer.

CHAPTER THREE

LACK OF INNER GAME

AVING LOOKED AT *The Queen*, a movie that had a solid Inner Game, let's now look at some films that didn't. It is, by the way, hard to come up with good examples—not because they're scarce (we see them at the theater and on TV constantly), but because they tend not to be terribly memorable.

First up is the science fiction action movie *Jumper*, starring Hayden Christensen. Christensen's character, David Rice, discovers at a young age that he can teleport. He puts this to good use, traveling the world, burglarizing bank vaults, and generally having a great time until he unfortunately finds himself the target of an ancient group that for centuries has sought out and killed teleporters because of a semi-religious conviction that human beings shouldn't possess that kind of power.

The Outer Game—trying to evade his pursuers and stay alive—leads to plenty of action and international scenery, with chase scenes jumping instantaneously from deserts to mountaintops, leading to a climax in which Rice kills his pursuer. So why did this big-budget feature gross less than its estimated budget of $85 million? You guessed it—not much of an Inner Game. To put it another way, our teleporter doesn't have a flaw to overcome.

The movie makes an attempt. The young version of the main character seems to be something of an outcast who has to grow up. And there are hints in there about his mother leaving the family when he was young. In fact, at the end of the movie, Christensen tracks down his mother, only to find that she is a member of the ancient anti-teleport group and that she left because she saw him teleport when he was a baby and didn't want to have to kill him. Cult memberships can be demanding.

None of it is terribly satisfying, even in a silly science fiction sort of way. More pointedly, the main character doesn't have a clear flaw that he has to overcome. If you love teleportation and electrified lariats, then this movie may be for you. But if you're interested in watching human beings evolve emotionally, you're pretty much out of luck. Even a silly movie like this one needs an Inner Game.

It's not just teen-targeted movies that can lack Inner Game. Take *Charlie Wilson's War*. With an estimated budget of $75 million, it only grossed a little more than $66 million domestically. Written by *West Wing* creator Aaron Sorkin, and starring Tom Hanks, Julia Roberts, and Philip Seymour Hoffman, it was markedly deficient in Inner Game.

The film is about Charlie Wilson (Hanks), a playboy congressman who gets involved in funding the anti-Soviet forces in post-invasion Afghanistan. This setup presents obvious potential for his character to develop: Wilson could go from uninformed, uncaring, uninvolved guy to expert agitator.

But, strangely, the screenplay goes out of its way to depict Hanks early on as pretty darn savvy. The unfortunate result of elevating the character early is to reduce the potential for change. The audience wants to see significant growth, from unhealthy to healthy—don't minimize it by starting the main character out too healthy.

The Outer Game, on the other hand, is fun. Will Wilson, along with Philip Seymour Hoffman's CIA agent and Julia Roberts' Texas socialite, be able to get funding for the Afghan mujahidin from Congress? It's a tough fight, but they get it done. But, again, the Inner Game just isn't there.

Take note: going-through-something is *not* Inner Game. Charlie Wilson definitely goes through something, and he accomplishes something, but he doesn't undergo a significant change, either for the better or for the worse. To sum up, *Charlie Wilson's War* has a decent Outer Game but no Inner Game. And there's no substitute for Inner Game.

Another "serious" movie that underperformed is *Michael Clayton*. It did okay at the box office, grossing just under $50 million on a budget of $25 million. But for a highly-praised film starring George Clooney and Tilda Swinton, who won an Oscar for playing the bad gal, it wasn't exactly a runaway hit. *Juno*, after all, grossed more than $140 million domestically ($230 million worldwide) on a budget of $7.5 million.

So let's look at *Michael Clayton*'s Inner Game. At the top of the film, Clayton is shown playing poker at an underground game. He doesn't seem to be enjoying himself much, but he doesn't seem manic or addicted, either. We then learn that he is the "fixer" for a law firm, helping their rich clients out when they have personal problems. He's not particularly happy, but his flaw, if he has one, is not obvious. Then he gets involved in a mystery that threatens his life.

By the end of the film, Clayton has turned the tables on evil corporate lawyer Karen Crowder (Swinton), who ordered the murder of Clayton's friend and tried to have Clayton killed as well. Again, an attempt is made to suggest that Clayton has evolved—he approaches Crowder with an offer to cover-up his friend's murder if she'll pay him several million dollars, but when she agrees to the deal, it turns that out he was broadcasting their conversation over his cell phone to the waiting police. She gets arrested and he doesn't get any money. There is some suggestion that he has changed, becoming the sort of person who won't take a multimillion-dollar payoff to cover up the murder of a good friend.

The problem is, he hasn't ever been set up as the kind of guy who would take a multimillion-dollar payoff to cover up the murder of a good friend. He's not portrayed as a saint, and there's something nonspecifically sleazy about his work for the law firm, but nothing even remotely as immoral as what he pretends to be doing at the end. So there's no believable change in the character. Again, Outer Game, but no Inner.

The same rule holds true for comedies—they need an Inner Game. Let's look, for example, at a successful romantic comedy, *Hitch*.

Will Smith stars as Alex "Hitch" Higgins, an anonymous dating consultant who helps men get dates with the women of their dreams. The Outer Game involves his helping an overweight accountant get a date with his celebrity client.

That Outer Game is cute, but the Inner Game, which entails inner growth for both Hitch and gossip columnist Sara Melas (Eva Mendes), is what made the movie work. Hitch is attracted to Sara, who is trying to find out who the secret dating consultant is, believing he was responsible for the humiliation of her friend.

In the end, Sara reawakens to the possibility of romance and Hitch learns that the real way to a woman's heart is to be himself. Both change for the better, and this strong Inner Game made the movie a big hit.

One final example to show that the Inner Game principle applies even to the silliest category of movies. When *Airplane!* was released, it was a huge hit, a brand-new kind of rapid-fire comedy that spawned a lot of similar films. Here's a question: Do you know what the Zucker Brothers' (the producers of *Airplane!*) next movie was? It wasn't *Airplane II*. It wasn't *The Naked Gun*, which was another big hit.

No, it was a film called *Top Secret!*, featuring the first movie role for a young Val Kilmer. It was not a hit. Yet the most brilliant comedy writer I know will tell you that, joke for joke, *Top Secret!* is a funnier movie than *Airplane!*. So why wasn't it as big a hit with audiences?

That's right, the Inner Game. As stupid as the Inner Game in *Airplane!* is —will pilot Ted Striker overcome his fear of flying and re-find love—and as much as the movie even makes fun of that story—it's just enough to work. And the same thing happens in *The Naked Gun*. As silly as the whole budding romance and "Nice beaver" dialog are, the audience cares enough about Lt. Frank Drebin to embrace his story, not just the jokes.

Top Secret!, on the other hand, doesn't have much of an Inner Game. It's a parody of Elvis Presley movies, which themselves are not known for strong Inner Games, and Kilmer plays an Elvis-type singer who becomes a spy for the U.S. while touring Europe during World War II. No Inner Game, really, at all. There are many brilliant comedy segments, but without a compelling Inner Game, the movie as a whole fell flat.

The point these films make is that even in this silliest of movie categories, the presence or absence of Inner Game can make the difference between success and failure. Don't misunderstand — no one's saying *Airplane!* succeeded because of its Inner Game, but *Top Secret!* failed because of its lack of one.

◆ ◆ ◆

In the next part of the book we'll look in more detail at the types of Inner Game.

EXERCISE

It's interesting to note that screenwriters often have an idea that their screenplay's Inner Game is lacking, so they'll hint at some elements, even if they don't develop them fully.

Screen *It's Complicated.* In that high-concept movie, Meryl Streep and Alec Baldwin play a divorced couple who get back together for an affair. There's some hiding, some pot smoking, but little Inner Game. Jane Adler (Streep) doesn't have a well-defined flaw to work through. But the film nonetheless includes scenes in which she gets together with her girlfriends to sorta-kinda discuss what's "wrong" with her. It's not enough to give the film a strong Inner Game, but you can see what the screenwriter was attempting by including it.

Part Two
THE TWO TYPES OF INNER GAME

Having been introduced to the concept of the Inner Game, some of you no doubt have thought of movies that seem not to fit the theory. How about *Alien*, for example? Who exactly overcomes an inner flaw while running from a murderous lizardoid in that successful film?

That's because Inner Games can be divided into two very different types: Morph and Myth. These two types work differently and give rise to very different types of movies.

Let's explore them in depth.

CHAPTER FOUR

THE MORPH ARCHETYPES

THE **Morph Archetype** is the sort we've been discussing, and it demonstrates the Inner Game literally: the audience watches an onscreen character—generally but not always the main character—go through an Outer Game adventure in order to deal with some psychological/emotional issues within themselves. They change—Morph—as we watch.

The three most common Morph Archetypes are **Evolution, Devolution,** and **Staying The Course.** Let's take a look at each of these to see how they work.

EVOLUTION

Evolution is undoubtedly the most common sort of script there is. It might be called a classic Hollywood movie, because it has a happy ending. But what that means in our context is, the Inner Game has a happy ending.

Here's how it works: a character (usually the main character) is set up at the beginning as having an inner flaw—maybe he's selfish or maybe she lacks self-confidence. The Outer Game comes along and throws this character's world out of balance, forcing him to deal with this inner flaw.

Why does he or she have to deal with it? That can vary from film to film. Maybe he has to overcome his inner flaw to gain what he's after in the Outer Game, or maybe she has to abandon what she's after in the Outer Game to overcome her flaw. Either way, the movie ends with the character having grown—Evolved—into a better person. Whether or not he attains the goal of the Outer Game is almost beside the point, and in different movies that can go either way. The important thing is the growth expressed in the Inner Game.

Remember that this brings up an obvious question: Why should this Evolution be satisfying for the audience? Because Evolution mirrors our common human experience—of overcoming our flaws and improving ourselves. I would go so far as to say that this is why people go to the movies, for this sort of Inner Game. Unlike a novel, a movie is so short that it has to focus—relentlessly—on this one important thing.

The Outer and Inner Games could be called the Head and the Heart of the movie. The Head is important, but what really sells the film to an audience is the Heart.

Let's look at some examples of Evolution screenplays. *Hancock* starts out introducing Will Smith as John Hancock, a homeless, alcoholic, one-time superhero who still occasionally tries to stop crimes but ends up causing more problems than he solves. There are issues with the film's middle section, but by the end of the movie, Hancock has clearly Evolved—he has stopped drinking himself into a stupor and has become a full-fledged, beloved superhero. True Evolution, and satisfying for the audience.

As an aside, let's mention that *occasionally* it's a character other than the main character who Evolves. Usually when that happens it's because the main character is already pretty close to perfect. He's what screenwriting teacher John Truby calls a "traveling angel." A character like Forrest Gump starts the movie so good that he doesn't have any flaws to overcome. But the secondary characters played by Gary Sinise and Robin Wright in that movie undergo profound changes, motivated by their interactions with Forrest. Same with the characters around Ferris Bueller or Crocodile Dundee or, more literally, on the TV shows *Highway to Heaven* or *Touched by an Angel*.

In *Touched by an Angel*, the main character is, literally, an angel, and every week she aids a human character who is going through a difficult period and needs help to Evolve. This series is a pure example of stories in which the guest characters Evolve, helped by the (unchanging) main character.

As a general rule, if you find that your main character isn't the one undergoing the most significant change, you should ask yourself if you've chosen the right main character. But sometimes it works, as the examples above demonstrate.

DEVOLUTION

The next Morph subtype is the—much rarer—**Devolution** archetype. In this type of story, the main character starts out healthy, but through the course of the screenplay he Devolves or sinks, ending up at a lower level than where he was at the beginning. It's the opposite of Evolution: he doesn't overcome his flaw; he succumbs to it.

The Devolution Inner Game is much less common than the Evolution Inner Game, but it can work, and garner audience acclaim. Why? While Evolution represents the audience's aspirations for positive change, Devolution provides them with a cautionary tale—just as we all hope to get better, we also fear we could get worse. An audience can enjoy watching a character Devolve, perhaps feeling good about avoiding that danger themselves. And critics like it because it's different from the usual Evolution movies they're forced to watch day in and day out.

The truly great example of Devolution remains *The Godfather*. When we first meet Michael Corleone, played by Oscar-nominated Al Pacino, he is a decorated Marine who has escaped the family business of organized crime. He's cheerful, he's successful, he has a pretty girlfriend (Diane Keaton). But when his father is shot and his big brother riddled with bullets, to save his family Michael becomes a criminal and a murderer. He succeeds in saving his family, but in the process sacrifices his soul.

To see that this is what the movie is "really about," it's interesting to see how often the movie goes back to it. In the middle of the film there's a sequence in which Michael makes a futile attempt to get back to a happy, non-criminal life. After he guns down the rival gangster and a New York police captain, he flees to Sicily, where he falls in love with a beautiful local girl. He marries her and would be happy to spend the rest of his life with her there. But again the criminal life intrudes when an attempt to assassinate him kills his bride instead. Michael returns to the U.S. and prepares to takes his father's place.

Later he gets his brother-in-law to confess to helping their rivals kill Michael's brother by assuring him that he would never consider harming his nephew's father, making him an orphan, after which he has him garroted. As the movie closes, Michael denies this murder to his wife and is greeted reverently as the new Godfather, his Devolution complete.

A couple more examples of Devolution. In *Thief*, James Caan plays Frank, a professional thief looking to get out of the business after one big score. But the criminal who finances his jobs won't let him retire, saying he doesn't fear Frank because he's become soft, lost his edge. To fight back, Frank has to Devolve back to the savage criminal he used to be, deliberately destroying everything he has so he can get back to that primal state.

In *The Candidate*, Robert Redford plays Bill McKay, an idealist who runs for U.S. Senate, not expecting to win, hoping only to use the campaign to publicize his ideas. But, under pressure from his staff and his own growing ambition, McKay compromises and Devolves so as not to lose. In the end, he wins the election, but winces at his Devolution, seemingly clueless about what he's going to do now that he's made the Big Show but lost his integrity in the process.

STAYING THE COURSE

The third major subtype of the Morph Inner Game is **Staying the Course**. In this Archetype, the main character neither Evolves nor Devolves — he remains essentially at the same level. It sounds like nothing much happens, so how can this subtype succeed, provide a satisfying story? What makes this work is that in order to Stay The Course, the character has to resist terrible temptations to Devolve.

Like Evolution, this is another popular story form because it's a common situation we all face: we have to resist the temptation to backslide, especially after we've worked through so much pain to improve ourselves. This variation is a trickier movie premise, because it's easier to depict progress than lack of regress.

For this reason, it's important to explicitly show the temptations the character resists. A good recent example is *300*. This huge international hit depicted how King Leonidas and a mere 300 Spartan warriors managed to hold off more than 100,000 Persians for several days in the Battle of Thermopylae in 480 BC. Although the Spartans were eventually overwhelmed by the Persians and slaughtered, they died glorious deaths and live in legend to this day.

300's Outer Game is the story of Leonidas (Gerard Butler) and his Spartans standing against the overwhelming Persian horde despite the prospect of certain death. The battles are exciting and the abdominal muscles phenomenal. But once again it is the Inner Game that begat the box office receipts.

And this Inner Game is markedly different in form from both Evolution and Devolution. The difference is that the main character hardly changes at all: Leonidas is as heroic at the beginning of the movie as he is at the end.

If one were trying to write this as an Evolution story, it would call for Leonidas to start, say, as a coward who grows and finds his inner hero.

But that's not what happens. Leonidas starts out heroic, killing a monstrous wolf as a young boy. He remains heroic, leading his men into battle against the Persian horde without hesitation, and finally dies heroic. Because in this variation the main character doesn't Evolve — instead he is faced with and resists temptations to Devolve; he Stays The Course.

Right off the bat the adult King Leonidas is approached by a Persian messenger, who tells him that if he'll agree to be ruled by the Persian demi-god Xerxes, he can keep Sparta and become even more powerful than he already is. Leonidas appears to think the offer over, then subtly indicates his rejection by kicking the messenger and his attendants into a bottomless well.

This temptation/rejection is repeated twice more. First, Leonidas meets Xerxes face-to-face, and Xerxes repeats his offer. This time Leonidas unhesitatingly rejects it, greatly angering the impressively muscular but sexually ambiguous god-king.

Finally, at the end of the film, Leonidas comes before Xerxes for the last time. The Persians have found a way to outflank the Spartans and are sure to kill them all if Leonidas fails to accept Xerxes' offer. And this time the offer is even sweeter—Leonidas and the Spartans have so impressed Xerxes with their semi-naked valor that if Leonidas will agree to worship and obey him, Leonidas will rule over not only Sparta but the rest of Persian-subjugated Greece as well.

And here's the screenwriters' brilliant stroke—it appears for a long moment that Leonidas will give in to the grotesque Persian leader. He takes off his helmet, throws down his shield and spear, and prostrates himself in the dirt before Xerxes.

But a second later he shouts an order to his men and we realize it's been a ruse. One of the Spartans kills a Persian spokesman and Leonidas himself flings his spear at Xerxes, cutting his cheek. Then Leonidas and his men fight and die, but die in glory.

And that is the key to Staying The Course: explicitly and repeatedly showing the main character's temptations to compromise. If he can resist, then the story will be satisfying, because even though the main character doesn't Evolve, he successfully resists Devolving.

It's important that the value being upheld in a Staying The Course screenplay be relatable to the audience. Take a look at *Redbelt*, written and directed by David Mamet. The main character is a master of Brazilian Jiu-Jitsu who is morally opposed to competing in the ring. When he is offered a spot in a tournament, he continually refuses, but eventually agrees because of debts that have piled up through no fault of his own.

At the last second, just before he is about to compete, he again refuses and instead fights his formidable opponent in the aisles of the arena, defeating him at the last moment. This conforms to the Staying The Course form, but it isn't very satisfying, because the value being protected—refusing to fight in the ring—isn't shared by the audience. You've got to assume that anyone going to a martial arts movie is there to see people fight onscreen, whether in a ring or not. So the main character's struggle not to compete doesn't land with much impact. It's better to stick with widely-held values like courage and honor.

A final example of Staying The Course is *Rudy*. In this film, Sean Astin plays Daniel "Rudy" Ruettiger, a Notre Dame fan who dedicates his life to getting admitted to the college and onto its football team, despite lacking obvious qualifications for either. Faced with setback after setback, he perseveres. He gets admitted to ND and walks on to be part of their scout team, the guys who give the varsity football players practice opponents but don't play in games.

Like King Leonidas, there's nothing really wrong with Rudy. He's impressively determined from the start, and there's no obvious Evolution for him to go through.

Being on the scout team is time-consuming and physically punishing for Rudy. When the coach who has promised him that he can suit up for the last game of his senior year leaves, and the new coach goes back on the promise, Rudy has had enough, and quits. But, like Leonidas rising from the ground, Rudy comes back, and his impressed teammates force the coach to let him suit up and take the field. In the end, he gets in for the game's (and his college career's) last two plays, sacks the opposing quarterback, and becomes the first Notre Dame player ever to be carried off the field, having truly Stayed The Course.

OTHER MORPH VARIATIONS

Before closing this chapter, it's worth looking at some other, less-frequently-seen variations on the Morph structure. These are constructed essentially by combining Evolution, Devolution, and Staying The Course, which makes sense because, after all, a character's psychological health can only go up, down, or sideways.

UNSUCCESSFUL EVOLUTION

First there's **Unsuccessful Evolution**. The main character starts out quite flawed, and then the Outer Game presents him with an opportunity to Evolve. He avails himself of the opportunity, though he may be somewhat ambivalent.

But, in the end, he fails to Evolve and instead falls back to his original state or even lower. His Evolution is unsuccessful.

A recent example of Unsuccessful Evolution is *The Wrestler*, which launched a comeback for star Mickey Rourke. Rourke plays Randy "The Ram" Robinson, a professional wrestler whose glory days are long behind him. He starts out pretty flawed — he's obsessed with his wrestling past, feeling it's the only thing that gives him value. Through the course of the movie, he is given the opportunity to Evolve: he gets a regular job, he gets closer to establishing a real relationship with his estranged daughter, and he makes progress winning over his stripper semi-girlfriend.

But, in the end, Randy refuses to embrace the possibilities of real life, and instead his obsession with his wrestling past wins out. He sinks lower than ever: he sacrifices his relationships with his daughter and his girl to remain a washed-up wrestler doing small shows in crummy gymnasiums, and — even worse — during the course of the screenplay he's had a heart attack and will probably die as a result of continuing.

Another example is *Leaving Las Vegas*. Nicolas Cage plays Ben Sanderson, an alcoholic who has lost everything and goes to Las Vegas, determined to drink himself to death. He forms a relationship with Sera, a troubled prostitute (Elisabeth Shue). Each tries to get the other to Evolve, and the audience hopes they'll succeed. In the end, however, Ben resists Evolution and dies, but there's still hope that Sera will Evolve.

FALL & REVIVAL

Next, there's **Fall & Revival**. In this type of screenplay, the main character first Devolves, and the question is whether he will Evolve enough to end up back at his original state.

Recent example: *An Education*. In this film, Jenny Mellor (Carey Mulligan), a bright but sheltered teenage girl, becomes the romantic target of David Goldman (Peter Sarsgaard), a 30-ish charmer, who introduces Jenny to a more affluent and adult world than she's ever experienced, much to her wide-eyed delight.

When David proposes marriage, she accepts, and drops out of school, to the disappointment of her teachers and family. But that is not Jenny's Devolution. Her Devolution occurs earlier, when she realizes that David is not a rich man of the world as he presents himself, but rather a con man and petty thief. It's in accepting this and continuing their relationship anyway, despite David's immorality, that Jenny Devolves.

The Outer Game turns, however, when Jenny stumbles onto the fact that David is already married. This causes her to break off the affair and starts her on the Evolution path back to her earlier state of being. She rejects David's immorality, and returns to her family and studies, completing the Revival story.

EVOLVE & MAINTAIN

The next example of a Morph variation can be found in *The Verdict*. In that film, down-on-his-luck, alcoholic lawyer Frank Galvin (Paul Newman) gets the opportunity to represent a comatose woman in a medical malpractice case that will net him easy money when he reaches a settlement with the Catholic diocese that runs the hospital. And he—desperately needing the money—is thrilled to do it.

But when he visits the poor victim and sees her lying in a hospital bed, all but dead, Galvin decides he can't go through with it. He rejects the low-ball settlement offer and opts to take the case to trial. He has Evolved, so the movie's over way too soon, right?

Wrong. If Galvin had truly and finally Evolved, if the Inner Game were completed, then, yes, the movie would be over prematurely. But the film actually segues into Staying The Course as we watch to see if he's going to backslide to his initial, flawed state. So this is not Evolution, it's **Evolve & Maintain**.

And, indeed, he begins to backslide right away. Difficulties with his case panic Galvin and he tries to reopen negotiations for a settlement. He's convinced he's going to lose. The Inner Game is by no means over — if anything, it seems highly unlikely that the early Evolution is going to stick. And the audience watches to see if it will.

In the end, Galvin wins the case and his Evolution appears to be permanent. He stops drinking, cleans up his act, and refuses to answer the phone call from his destructive girlfriend. The Evolution/Staying The Course combination works well in this film.

STAYING THE COURSE WITH A POP

The Dark Knight is a film that demonstrates how a screenwriter can give a Staying The Course movie a little Evolution pop at the end. *The Dark Knight* is set up as a Staying The Course story — The Joker (Heath Ledger) spends the film trying to get Batman (Christian Bale) to come down to his level and fight. Batman repeatedly resists this Devolution, thus Staying The Course.

But the movie doesn't end there — at the last moment, Batman goes even further. In order that the citizens of Gotham City not lose hope, he takes the blame for the murders committed by Harvey Dent (Aaron Eckhart), so no one will find out Dent has been corrupted by the Joker and turned into the evil Two-Face. At the last possible moment, Batman has not merely Stayed The Course, he has Evolved into an even better, self-sacrificing person. This is an exception to the rule that the Evolving character should start highly flawed. Since this is primarily a Staying The Course movie, Batman starts out good and stays good, becoming even better at the very end.

These variations can be very satisfying for the audience because they're different, less familiar. By combining the classic forms, a clever screenwriter can create something unique.

APPARENT EVOLUTION

The next type is based on the fact that a character's Evolution is seen from the audience's point of view. That means that a character need not *actually* change, so long as it appears to the audience that he has.

Take as an example *Eastern Promises*. In this film, Viggo Mortensen plays Nikolai Luzhin, a mobster's driver and body-disposer with the potential to advance within a Russian organized crime gang in London. Despite his occupation, Nikolai is likeable to the audience, and we wish he could Evolve. By the end of the film, Nikolai has killed his way to becoming the ultimate boss of the mob, but he is also revealed to be an undercover agent helping the British government infiltrate the criminals.

Of course, Nikolai hasn't really Evolved — he's been undercover the entire time — but because the audience didn't know what he was up to, he has *apparently* changed. From the audience's point of view, he's gone from murderous criminal to government crime fighter. And to the audience, this kind of apparent change can be as satisfying as if the character had actually Evolved.

Another example of this seldom-seen variation occurs in *The Usual Suspects*. Kevin Spacey stars as Roger "Verbal" Kint, a crippled, small-time conman being interrogated by a detective about a recent explosion that left more than two dozen men dead.

Verbal tells the detective a detailed story about an elaborate heist that went wrong. At the end of the interrogation, Verbal is released, but the detective realizes that the entire story he's just been told may have been a convoluted lie.

And we, the audience, see Spacey transform from the crippled Verbal to commanding super-criminal Keyser Söze. As with

Nikolai in *Eastern Promises*, Verbal has been faking the entire time, and his Evolution, though not actual, is apparent, and quite satisfying.

You'll notice that the use of Apparent Evolution relies on *concealment*. The character conceals his nature from the other characters in the story, and from the audience. When his true nature is eventually revealed, it has the same effect as conventional Evolution.

APPARENT DEVOLUTION

If you thought Apparent Evolution was a rare variation, here's one that's even more rare—**Apparent Devolution**.

Like Apparent Evolution, it relies on concealment. An example is *Training Day*, starring Denzel Washington and Ethan Hawke. Hawke plays Jake Hoyt, a young cop on his first day as an undercover narcotics officer, riding with Det. Alonzo Harris (Washington), the commanding officer of the unit. Over the course of the film, Harris' true nature is gradually revealed, apparently Devolving.

At first, Harris seems to be an unconventional cop, willing to break the rules, but ultimately interested in enforcing the law and getting drugs and drug dealers off the street. But as the story progresses, we see his dark side emerge—he and his men murder and rob a drug dealer so that Harris can pay off a gambling debt, and when Hoyt balks at going along with his commanding officer's schemes, Harris hires some gang members to murder him. Again, Harris does not change—he is concealing his true nature, from both Hoyt and the audience—but the gradual revelation of the truth is perceived by the audience as Devolution.

FIDDLING WITH THE TIMELINE

This is not an Archetype, but rather another aspect to Apparent Evolution. Screenwriters will sometimes deliberately show scenes out of chronological order. Does it "work"? Sometimes it does, and sometimes it doesn't. The key is whether or not the distortion of time contributes to the appearance of Evolution.

A prominent pioneer in this is *Pulp Fiction*. Here, John Travolta and Samuel L. Jackson portray Vincent Vega and Jules Winnfield, hit men who start the movie by killing a group of thieves who have stolen something from their gangster boss. They then accidentally kill their driver and have to call a man who helps them clean up the mess.

Then they go to eat at a diner, where two patrons attempt to rob the customers. Vincent and Jules overpower the robbers, but spare their lives, and Jules decides to leave the criminal life and become a better person. Vincent goes out with the boss' wife and revives her when her heart stops after a drug overdose. When the boss sends Vincent to kill Butch, a boxer who double-crossed him after promising to throw a match, Butch instead kills Vincent, then goes on to save the boss from being raped.

All in all, not a very coherent Evolution story. So screenwriter/director Quentin Tarantino cuts the story up and shows it out of chronological order, ending it on Vincent and Jules sparing the diner robbers and walking out of the diner. Because of the altered timeline, it has the effect on the audience of Apparent Evolution.

Contrast that with *Rendition*. In this film, Reese Witherspoon plays an American woman whose Egyptian-born husband is suspected of being involved in a terrorist bombing, seized returning from a foreign conference, and sent to a secret facility in the Middle East, where he is interrogated and tortured.

The relevant point to this discussion is that there is another storyline in which the interrogator/torturer's daughter runs away with her boyfriend, who, unbeknownst to her, is a terrorist. At the end of the movie it's revealed that this storyline, which has appeared to be running concurrently with the interrogation storyline, in fact occurred previously, with the bombing that ends the runaway daughter story the same bombing that initiates the interrogation/torture story.

But this time warp—unlike the one in *Pulp Fiction*—has no point. It doesn't further any aspect of the Inner Game in any way. It's simply done to be clever, to tell the audience, "You thought you understood what was going on, but I fooled you."

It didn't make the movie any better, and it didn't make the movie any more popular. Don't tell the audience you're smarter than they are—it'll only put them off.

◆ ◆ ◆

So that is the list of Morph Inner Game Archetypes available to the screenwriter. The next chapter will discuss the other kind of Inner Game Archetypes: Myth.

EXERCISE

A "log line" is the one-sentence description of a movie. Any writer will tell you that a good log line is essential to selling the idea, and marketing executives will tell you that a good log line is vital to getting people to buy tickets.

In a Morph screenplay, it's important to both describe the Outer Game and hint at the Inner Game. So, for example, if you're writing a log line for *Free Willy*, don't just write *"A boy befriends an ill-fated killer whale.*" That gives no hint to the Inner Game. Instead, go with something like this actual *Free Willy* log line from DirecTV: *"An abandoned boy with a chip on his shoulder befriends an ill-fated killer whale."* That log line gives the audience an idea of the main character's inner flaw, and, since they've seen movies before, an idea of the Evolution Inner Game of the film.

On the other hand, it's important to not go too far in describing the Inner Game. For example, here's the DirecTV log line for *Love Happens*, starring Jennifer Aniston and Aaron Eckhart: *"A self-help guru comes to the realization that he has never confronted the loss of his wife."* This log line is pure Inner Game without even a hint of what Jennifer Aniston is doing in the movie. It fails to set up the Outer Game at all.

EXERCISE

Write log lines for the movies *The Queen*, *Hancock*, *Crocodile Dundee*, and *Tootsie*. Be sure to both describe the Outer Game and hint at the Inner Game by mentioning the inner flaw of the character who will Evolve.

CHAPTER FIVE

USING THE ENNEAGRAM TO CONSTRUCT MORPH INNER GAMES

UP TO THIS POINT, we've focused on the Morph Archetypes, in which a character has an inner flaw that he overcomes as a result of going through the Outer Game.

But how do you come up with that inner flaw? The danger is that the screenwriter will just throw a flaw onto a generic character, making for an unconvincing fit. Is there something that will help in this process?

The **Enneagram** can help.

The Enneagram is a personality classification system that divides people into nine personality types, going into these types in great detail. Their hopes and dreams, their characteristics and fears. But especially helpful for screenwriters, it outlines healthy and unhealthy versions of each type. As a result, it meshes beautifully with the theory set forth in this book, giving clear and believable examples of Evolution and Devolution for each type.

The Enneagram types are the following (note that there are no official names, and different books use different terminology):

Type 1   The Reformer
Type 2   The Helper
Type 3   The Achiever
Type 4   The Individualist
Type 5   The Investigator
Type 6   The Loyalist
Type 7   The Enthusiast
Type 8   The Challenger
Type 9   The Peacemaker

It's important to realize that no Type is either good or bad. Every Type comes in healthier and less healthy versions.

Other screenwriting books, like Jeff Kitchen's *Writing a Great Movie*, have recommended the Enneagram as a tool for coming up with complex, believable characters. This chapter will touch on that, but go more deeply into using the Enneagram to construct a Morph Inner Game. It can be an amazing tool for screenwriters.

Let's take a Type often used in screenwriting, Type 8: The Challenger. Here's the short description from the extremely useful website of the Enneagram Institute (*www.enneagraminstitute.com*):

> The powerful, aggressive type. Eights are self-confident, strong, and assertive. Protective, resourceful, straight-talking, and decisive, but can also be egocentric and domineering. Eights

feel they must control their environment, especially people, sometimes becoming confrontational and intimidating. Eights typically have problems with their tempers and with allowing themselves to be vulnerable. At their Best: self-mastering, they use their strength to improve others' lives, becoming heroic, magnanimous, and inspiring.

Again, it's worth repeating that Eights—like all other Types—are neither good nor bad in themselves. Eights can be presidents, or they can be bank robbers—it just depends on how healthy or unhealthy they are. But they share their basic characteristics with other Eights.

In Morph screenplays, this can help the screenwriter come up with the main character's "flaw." Often, screenwriters don't come up with a terribly convincing flaw. They'll construct a flat, generic character and then make him selfish or mean or withdrawn or whatever the plot calls for. The Enneagram lets you build the flaw in while you're creating the character.

Let's take a look at how you could do this for a Type 8 main character. We'll start him out at a fairly low level of health:

> **Level 7:** Defying any attempt to control them, become completely ruthless, dictatorial, "might makes right." The criminal and outlaw, renegade, and con-artist. Hard-hearted, immoral and potentially violent.

Now, let's take a look at a fairly healthy version:

> **Level 2:** Self-assertive, self-confident, and strong; have learned to stand up for what they need and want. A resourceful, "can-do" attitude and passionate inner drive.

Equipped with these two descriptions, it's straightforward to make the "flawed" main character initially an unhealthy (Level 7) Type 8 and let him Evolve into a healthier (Level 2) Type 8 through the course of the screenplay. The flaw won't feel like it's just stuck on, because it's an integral part of the main character's personality.

Looking for examples of this technique in the world of produced movies can be difficult. After all, most screenplays are written without resorting to the Enneagram. But some fit in quite well, so let's take a look.

Since we're talking about Type 8, let's look again at *300*. In that film, Leonidas is king of Sparta when a seemingly unbeatable Persian horde approaches to attack and destroy. Leonidas decides to fight.

As previously pointed out, *300* is not a typical Evolution movie; instead it's a Staying The Course movie. So Leonidas — very much a Type 8 — doesn't change from an unhealthy Type 8 to a healthy one. He starts and finishes as a healthy, brave Type 8.

So how can using the Enneagram help a screenwriter sitting down to write *300*? Take a look at this passage from the Enneagram Institute's website:

> When Eights are emotionally healthy, however, they have a resourceful, "can-do" attitude as well as a steady inner drive. They take the initiative and make things happen with a great passion for life. They are honorable and authoritative — natural leaders who have a solid, commanding presence. *Their groundedness gives them abundant "common sense" as well as the ability to be decisive. Eights are willing to "take the heat," knowing that any decision cannot please everyone. But as much as possible, they want to look after the interests*

of the people in their charge without playing favorites. They use their talents and fortitude to construct a better world for everyone in their lives. [emphasis added]

Here's an example of how using this Enneagram information could help a screenwriter in constructing this story. In the course of the movie, Leonidas is approached by the deformed hunchback Ephialtes. Ephialtes is a Spartan, but he wasn't allowed to serve in the army because of his disability. He begs Leonidas to allow him to serve with the 300.

Leonidas listens to Ephialtes' request quite respectfully and watches as Ephialtes rather impressively displays his self-taught weaponry skills. We get the feeling he's going to grant Ephialtes his request.

But then he asks the deformed Spartan to demonstrate the movements and positions he would need to serve, not as an individual, but as part of the Spartan unit. And because of his condition, Ephialtes can't do what he would have to do. Leonidas regretfully tells him that because of that, he won't be allowed to serve.

Leonidas is absolutely right — Ephialtes' presence in the Spartan corps would endanger the other soldiers. And because Leonidas is a healthy Type 8, he has to do what is right. Not what might feel good at the moment, but what's right. And what is right is to disappoint Ephialtes and not endanger the other men.

If you were setting out to write this story, you might not think of this episode. You might just have Ephialtes be mad at Leonidas and the Spartans for something and let that be his motivation for helping the Persians. But referring to the Enneagram description might give you the idea: since you're depicting Leonidas as a healthy Type 8 who refuses to Devolve, why not explore other aspects of that Type. Why not explore his absolute fairness and unwillingness to compromise what he knows to be right.

And the episode with Ephialtes is important in the Outer Game, too. After being turned down by Leonidas, Ephialtes is bribed and flattered by the Persians so he will reveal to them the hidden way through the mountains, the secret route that will allow them to outflank the Spartans and get behind them. So picking an Enneagram Type and then exploring its intricacies is a great way to get not just character, but plot.

The point is to translate the rule to "Give the character an inner flaw and let him overcome it" into the Enneagram-based version: "Let the character start as an unhealthy version of his Enneagram type and evolve into a healthier version."

You can find short descriptions of the Enneagram Types from The Enneagram Institute online at *www.enneagraminstitute.com*. The Institute offers a number of other articles and aids that are very helpful for screenwriters. I especially recommend their Enneagram Charts and their classic book *Personality Types* by Don Richard Riso with Russ Hudson.

I also recommend that you consider buying the Enneagram Institute's online test, both because it's enlightening to learn about yourself and because it will give you access to their Expanded Enneagram Type Descriptions. These will give screenwriters advice like "Eights grow by recognizing that the world is not a battleground to be approached as a gigantic test of wills," and they can be enormously helpful in plotting out your Morph screenplays.

Getting back to using the Enneagram, the challenge is to translate our basic premise into the language of the Enneagram. Our general model is the Morph screenplay of the Evolution variety.

We start with a main character who has a psychological/emotional flaw. As a result of being put through the Outer Game, the character manages to overcome his flaw and end up a better person. Now let's translate that into Enneagram-speak.

The main character, like everyone, has an Enneagram type. The screenwriter picks the Type that will work best in his or her story. For example, if the character has to learn that money isn't everything, he should probably start out as someone who believes that money *is* everything, that material possessions are very, very important. A natural choice would be a Type 3:

> Threes are self-assured, attractive, and charming. Ambitious, competent, and energetic, they can also be status-conscious and highly driven for advancement. They are diplomatic and poised, but can also be overly concerned with their image and what others think of them.

Next, it's an Evolution story, so the character should start in a relatively unhealthy state. Take a look at Level 7:

> **Level 7:** Fearing failure and humiliation, they can be exploitative and opportunistic, covetous of the success of others, and willing to do "whatever it takes" to preserve the illusion of their superiority.

So, following through with this exercise, we start with a status-conscious Type 3 who is exploitative and opportunistic. He is put through an Outer Game that "teaches him a lesson" and leaves him a healthier version of his Type 3 self. For example:

> **Level 2:** Self-assured, energetic, and competent with high self-esteem: they believe in themselves and their own value. Adaptable, desirable, charming, and gracious.

That, in a nutshell, is how the Enneagram can be a highly useful tool for the screenwriter. In simplest terms, it replaces the fuzzy phrases "has a flaw" and "overcomes his flaw" with the more precise Enneagram terms "starts at an unhealthy level" and "ends at a healthier level."

Let's see this at work. In *Wall Street*, Charlie Sheen plays Bud Fox, a struggling stockbroker who desperately craves material success and status. In other words, he is an unhealthy Type 3.

He doesn't care how he achieves his goal. I suppose if he were genuinely good at figuring out which stocks are going to go up, he'd use that to gain money and status and would end up a productive member of society. But he's not, so he breaks into offices after hours and goes through their files, looking for opportunities for illegal insider trading. As the Type 3 description says, the important thing to him is maintaining image, whatever that takes.

His father (Martin Sheen) is the one who tells him that this is no way to live, that there are things more important in life than money. Bud has to make a choice between his real father and his surrogate father, evil tycoon Gordon Gekko (Michael Douglas).

For most of the movie he follows Gekko, but, in the end, he listens to his real father and Evolves. He turns both himself and Gekko in to the authorities, condemning both of them to prison. He has Evolved from an unhealthy Type 3 to a healthy Type 3.

So that's the Enneagram approach: find an Enneagram type for the character so that the flaw he or she will overcome is embodied in an unhealthy version of that Type. As the screenplay progresses, show the character moving back and forth between healthier and less-healthy versions. Then, in an Evolution story, let him or her make the final move to the healthier version.

Again, using a comprehensive psychological tool like the Enneagram will lend a feeling of authenticity to this process, because the Types are real and they're consistent.

Make sure you don't try to change the character's Enneagram Type altogether. That doesn't happen in real life, and you shouldn't try to make it happen in your screenplay. No one changes from a success-oriented Type 3 to a self-effacing Type 9. People remain the same Type but have the opportunity to become healthier versions of it.

An obvious point—the Enneagram can of course also be used for other Morph Archetypes, like Devolution and Staying The Course. In a Devolution story, the character will start as a relatively healthy version of his Enneagram type and fall to an unhealthy version. And in a Staying The Course story, the character will start relatively healthy and resist falling to an unhealthy version.

So using the Enneagram to structure your Inner Game will help you make your character's Evolution significant, but still believable.

In sum, the Enneagram provides a brilliant tool for screenwriters seeking to create consistent, believable characters and involving, moving Inner Games. By the way, it's also a fun way to learn something about yourself and maybe make yourself a better person.

EXERCISE

Screen episodes of *The Sopranos* and *House*. These two shows will be discussed later in the Television section, but the important thing to note here is how the structures are similar but the shows totally different

Both shows revolve around a main character with a flaw, and that main character could get better or worse as the series goes on. That's the similarity, but the difference is huge.

Tony Soprano is a Type 8: The Challenger — powerful and dominating, self-confident, decisive, willful, and confrontational. Gregory House is a Type 5: The Investigator — intense and cerebral, perceptive, innovative, secretive, and isolated. They're both such perfect examples of their Types that it's quite possible the producers referred to the Enneagram when creating the shows.

Read the short descriptions of these Types at *www. enneagraminstitute.com*. Make a list of examples of how each character Evolves and Devolves in episodes of their shows.

CHAPTER SIX

THE MYTH ARCHETYPES

THE OTHER CATEGORY OF ARCHETYPES is that of **Myth Archetypes**. They provide other stories that audiences love and are very different from the Morph Archetypes in the way they handle Inner Game.

Recall that in the Morph screenplay, the Inner Game is presented *directly*: the audience watches the main character as he goes through the Outer Game and at the same time goes through the Inner Game, either Evolving, Devolving, Staying The Course, or a combination of those.

The Myth Archetype works quite differently. The main character goes through the Outer Game, and that Outer Game *symbolizes* the Inner Game. If that sounds confusing, don't worry—examples will make it clear.

The screenwriter can't write just any Morph-free story and say it's Myth—there are several *specific* types of Myth stories that have symbolic resonance. The first Archetype and its variations symbolically echo the Morph Archetypes we've already dealt with.

MONSTER

Monster stories have been popular for centuries. How do they work? Initially, a monster of some kind menaces the hero and the community. In *Beowulf*, the village is threatened by Grendel. In the first James Bond movie, *Dr. No*, the world is threatened by a monstrous supervillain. The monster can be a real monster, as in *Alien*; a monstrous animal, as in *Jaws*; a monstrous human, like Glenn Close's character in *Fatal Attraction*; an evil horde like the Persians in *300*; even a disease or disaster threatening the main character or all of mankind.

The main character fights against the seemingly unbeatable monster, losing most of the battles until it looks like he has no hope and will ultimately lose the war. But, in the end, through superhuman effort, the main character manages to overcome the monster and "kill" it in some way. Not necessarily kill literally, but nullify somehow.

These Myth stories work well. They've been around a long time and audiences still flock to them. But they often feature a main character who undergoes little or no inner change. So how can we square this with the theory that a screenplay succeeds or fails based on its Inner Game?

Here's how: In Monster stories, the Outer Game *symbolizes* the Inner Game. The monster symbolizes a human fault that the main character has to overcome. Killing the monster is a symbol for overcoming the flaw and Evolving.

What fault does the monster symbolize? There are at least three theories of how that works. In his book *The Seven Basic Plots*, Christopher Booker asserts that the monster always symbolizes human egocentricity. By defeating the monster, the hero symbolically Evolves by defeating the egocentricity within all of us.

It's important that the monster really be monstrous. Writing a Monster screenplay isn't simply a way to dispense with Inner Game. It's not enough, for example, to try to defeat an opponent in a sporting event—you have to make the opponent a monster. In *Rocky*, Rocky Balboa's opponent Apollo Creed is a trash-talker, but in no way a monster, so the movie succeeds because of Rocky's Evolution. In the sequels *Rocky III* and *Rocky IV*, Rocky's opponents *are* monsters—Clubber Lang because he kills Rocky's trainer, and Ivan Drago because he kills Apollo Creed (having the monster kill a beloved character is a great way to make him or it more monstrous)—so these films work as Monster stories. Make sure you make your monsters really, really bad. The more people they threaten, and the worse the threats are, the more effective your monsters will be.

If the monster isn't immediately threatening, it can be hard to make the story work. In *Invictus*, starring Morgan Freeman and Matt Damon, the main characters—Freeman's Nelson Mandela and Damon's rugby player—don't Evolve, and the movie seems intended to be a Monster story. If South Africa's national rugby team can win the 1995 Rugby World Cup, it will unite the country and kill the monster of apartheid. But the monster by that time has become somewhat abstract, and it's not completely convincing that winning the big rugby game will kill it. The movie took in only $37 million domestically on a budget of $60 million.

A second theory is that the monster symbolizes a more specific human fault present in the story's setup. In *Jaws*, for example, the reason the town won't close the beaches when the shark starts eating bathers is greed: they know they should close them, but they don't want to lose money due to lost tourism. By this theory, the fault the shark symbolizes is greed. In truth, though, once the main protagonists start fighting the shark out on the open water, any feeling that the shark symbolizes greed quickly disappears.

Along similar lines, in any of the many films in which a corrupt man says "I am a United States Senator!", the flaw can be seen as general abuse of power.

A third theory—and this can really work well in some movies—is that the monster is less general and more specific to the main character. In *Taken*, Bryan Mills (Liam Neeson) fights Eastern European gangsters and an Arab sheikh to save his daughter, who has been kidnapped to be addicted to drugs and sold into sexual slavery. By the second theory, the monstrous villains might represent something along the lines of social mistreatment of women.

But in the film, Mills is trying to redeem himself for neglecting his family during his younger years due to his demanding CIA superspy career. By this third theory, the monstrous slaver gang would symbolize the damage caused by his paternal neglect of his daughter. After all, prostitution can be seen as the exaggerated version of the dangerous, promiscuous lifestyle that neglected daughters can fall into.

Whatever the theory, the hero's battle with the monster *symbolizes* his battle with an inner flaw, and his final triumph over the beast symbolizes his Evolution. Or his final defeat symbolizes his Devolution.

The latter is what happens in *No Country for Old Men*. Llewelyn Moss (Josh Brolin) stumbles onto a pile of money after a drug deal goes bad and helps himself to it. From then on, he is pursued by monster Anton Chigurh (Javier Bardem), an unstoppable, heartless killing machine who's been hired to retrieve the cash. Out of sheer self-preservation, Moss does his best to defeat Chigurh.

But in keeping with the Coen Brothers' sensibility, Moss ends up dead instead of triumphant. Strangely, Moss isn't killed by Chigurh, the monster, but by some anonymous bad guys the audience never really knows, and off-screen to boot. Highly unusual for a Monster movie, which may explain why despite winning four Oscars, including Best Picture and Best Adapted Screenplay, the movie topped out with box office receipts of only around $75 million domestically.

When you're writing a Monster screenplay, it's best to keep the story straightforward—don't give the audience unnecessary information. In *Lakeview Terrace*, Samuel L. Jackson plays a scary cop who terrorizes the interracial couple that moves in next door, and they're forced to fight back. A promising Monster setup, but the film confuses matters by taking pains to tell us a couple of things: that the husband isn't such a great guy, and that Jackson's monster has his reasons for being a psycho. These dissipate the movie's impact—would it really help *Jaws* if we knew that the shark had a bad childhood?

NICE MONSTER

Monster variation movies like *Frankenstein* and *King Kong* start out in standard fashion—a hideous, scary monster is introduced and starts to wreak havoc on the human community. But partway into the movie, the audience gets the message that the monster isn't so bad. Indeed it seems to be better—more human—than the actual humans trying to kill it. I call this **Nice Monster**.

Kong, for example, is exploited by the evil hunters and showmen who kidnap the giant gorilla from his island. He loves the beautiful Ann Darrow and protects her from pushy dinosaurs. He protects her right up to the moment he's shot and plunges from the Empire State Building to his death. To put it simply, he's not very monstrous; he's actually kind of sweet.

This switcheroo tends to muddle the symbolic Inner Game. Not being so bad, the monster no longer coherently symbolizes an inner flaw, so the audience unconsciously tries to reconstruct the narrative in a way that makes Inner Game sense. It doesn't always succeed. The latest version of *King Kong* grossed a little more than $200 million domestically, but with a budget also a bit over $200 million, it wasn't exactly a rousing commercial success.

RUN AWAY!

Given the symbolism of the Monster story, it's important to avoid certain pitfalls. One is the misuse of what I call a **Run Away!** story, a story form that usually doesn't work. Recent examples of this are *War of the Worlds*, *The Happening*, and *2012*.

In *War of the Worlds*, Ray Ferrier (Tom Cruise) spends the movie running to escape an overwhelming alien invasion. Sure, the military is futilely trying to kill the aliens and their deadly machines. But Ferrier isn't — he's just running away.

This is not to criticize the fictional character — in real life, if you encounter a technologically advanced alien invasion, I'm advising you to run away. But it doesn't work as symbolism: you can't overcome your inner flaw by running away from it. Wherever you run, your inner flaw stays right with you. In a Monster story, the character can try to escape the monster at first, but he must eventually realize that that's not going to work and turn his attention to killing it.

That's what happens in *Duel*, Steven Speilberg's breakthrough TV movie. David Mann (Dennis Weaver) is a motorist tormented by an unidentifiable truck driver, who pursues him relentlessly. Mann spends most of the film trying to get away from the truck, but, in the end, when he realizes he can't escape, he turns and fights and kills his tormentor.

And remember the turning point in *The Matrix*. The humans must constantly flee from the all-powerful agents, but at the climax of the movie, Neo (Keanu Reeves) instead turns to do battle with Agent Smith (Hugo Weaving). He has realized he must kill the monster, and Morpheus (Laurence Fishburne) marks the realization by saying "He's starting to believe." Neo kills the monster and saves humanity from the Matrix.

By way of contrast, in *War of the Worlds*, the aliens eventually succumb to earthly bacteria, so the final symbolic message is something like "If you run from your inner flaw, you might get lucky and it will go away on its own." Not quite as inspirational as "If you battle your inner demon, you can defeat it."

The Happening has the same problem. Elliot Moore (Mark Wahlberg) runs away from another monster, this time an airborne disease that causes people to commit suicide. He and a few others run and run and run. . . and eventually the disease stops. They've outrun the monster. Again, symbolically (you can outrun your inner flaw) unsatisfying.

Finally, look at *2012*—it has exactly the same problem. Jackson Curtis (John Cusack) stumbles onto an impending disaster—neutrinos are causing the earth to heat up and melt the crust layer we all live on. He manages to pick up his family in a limousine so they can escape the devastation and sneak onto giant arks the world's governments have built to save a select few.

In this movie, too, the monster just goes away. Once the melting has caused massive earthquakes and tidal waves, the damage is done and the survivors just have to wait on the giant boats for a few years until the water recedes. Yet another symbolically unsatisfying message: "Avoid your inner flaw long enough — it will do a lot of damage, but ultimately someone else will save you."

Maybe the symbolism issue is why *The Blair Witch Project* — which also employed Run Away! — did succeed, becoming the most successful movie, based on cost, in history. A group of documentarians hiking through the woods find that they're being tracked by a seemingly supernatural predator. They try to flee, but they can't get away, and in the end they're all caught and killed. This time, the Run Away! symbolism actually works: if you simply try to run away from your inner flaws, you won't escape them, and eventually they'll destroy you.

This same thing works in *Cloverfield*. A group of twenty-somethings flee for their lives from a giant creature that is laying waste to Manhattan. As in *Blair Witch*, it's all being caught on someone's videotape. And in the end, again as in *Blair Witch*, they all end up dead, killed by the monster.

Cloverfield was another box office success, grossing more than $80 million ($170 worldwide) on an estimated budget of $25 million. So Run Away! can work, but only if the screenwriter follows through with the Archetype's symbolism and lets the monster kill the characters in the end.

WRONG MONSTER

Another example of a variation on Monster is offered by *Basic Instinct*. Sharon Stone portrays the genital-flashing, murderous monster Catherine Trammel, being tracked by detective Nick Curran (Michael Douglas). But Nick gets tricked by Catherine into believing that Beth Garner (Jeanne Tripplehorn), the police psychologist Nick occasionally has rough sex with, is the actual killer, and he shoots her dead. In other words, Nick kills the wrong monster.

In the final scene, Nick is in bed with Catherine, and we see her ice pick on the floor underneath. Seems like it's not going to work out for our protagonist, which is symbolically appropriate—if instead of solving your actual inner problem you solve another problem you think you have (but don't), you're not going to get any better. A fascinating variation on Monster—**Wrong Monster**.

A similar dynamic occurs in *Mystic River*. Jimmy Markum (Sean Penn) comes to believe that his daughter has been murdered by his childhood friend Dave Boyle (Tim Robbins), so he murders Boyle in retaliation. Then Markum finds out his daughter was killed by someone else. He's killed the wrong monster. As the movie ends, we're sure Markum is in for more trouble as a result of what he's done.

KILLED BY THE MONSTER

A final example of a Monster variation is one that doesn't work very well. In *Valkyrie*, Tom Cruise plays Colonel Claus von Stauffenberg, a German officer who mounts a plot to assassinate Adolf Hitler and free Germany from the Nazi regime.

The conspirators do eventually set off an explosion, but Hitler survives and all are executed, including Von Stauffenberg, who is shot by a firing squad.

Valkyrie barely outgrossed its estimated budget domestically, chiefly because of its handling of the Monster Archetype. Von Stauffenberg does everything he can to kill the monster (Hitler), but in the end the monster kills him. The unfortunate symbolic message is that you can fight your inner flaw, but sometimes it's just too strong to defeat, and instead it defeats you. Not very inspiring, and not very lucrative at the box office.

The Monster Archetype and its variations correspond to the Evolution/Devolution Archetypes quite closely. But there are other types of Myth Archetypes that do not. Next we turn to some Myth Inner Games that symbolize stories other than Evolution and Devolution.

CINDERELLA

The first of these is **Cinderella**. The Cinderella story is symbolic not of overcoming an inner flaw, but of something else — the universal experience of growing from child to adult.

In a Cinderella story, the main character is sometimes introduced as an actual child, but more often as a child-like person, poor or otherwise in a bad situation and lacking the qualities of an adult. She or he is not flawed so much as oppressed, oppressed by adult characters — just as all children feel oppressed by their parents — along with favored peers who represent privileged siblings. As the story progresses, he or she develops — usually helped by a supportive adult (the Fairy Godmother) — and in the end overcomes the parental and fraternal oppression and stands fully developed, not Evolved but rather finally liberated and revealed, exhibiting the wonderful qualities hidden within from the beginning.

Symbolic of the main character's having grown up and become an independent adult.

One form of Cinderella, of course, is present in all the variations of the Cinderella fairy tale, as well as books and movies like *Great Expectations*. But it sometimes makes an appearance in less-expected places.

Consider, for example, *The Bourne Identity*. Jason Bourne (Matt Damon) is fished out of an amniotic sea at the beginning (re-Bourne?), for all practical purposes an infant, unable even to care for himself. He can't remember who he is, though his CIA handlers do and seek to control him and send his brother assassins (think evil stepsisters) to kill him. Throughout the movie, Bourne shows flashes of what he's capable of and eventually defeats the parental and fraternal pressure and emerges as the world's most dangerous assassin. Who knew a Cinderella story could be so much fun for guys?

Or consider *A Knight's Tale*. Heath Ledger plays William Thatcher, a commoner who pretends to be noble knight Sir Ulrich von Lichtenstein so he can compete in jousting tournaments. He travels through England with his friends, including Geoffrey Chaucer, going from tournament to tournament.

Being a commoner isn't a flaw, and *A Knight's Tale* is not an Evolution story. When William stands revealed at the end of the film as a jousting champion and bona fide knight, it is the end of a Cinderella story—he has simply become and been revealed as what he has potentially been. He was always capable of being a knight; it was the rest of society that had to catch up.

And there's a final, fascinating parallel between *A Knight's Tale* and the Cinderella fairy tale. At one point William's archrival,

Count Adhemar, discovers William's humble birth and exposes him, causing William to be arrested and put in the stocks. Entertainment-starved townspeople understandably gather to pelt him with rotting vegetables. His situation seems hopeless.

But he is saved. Who saves him? The handsome prince. Earlier in the story, William has shown Prince Edward a kindness, by jousting with him when the other knights, on finding out he was royalty despite his disguise, frustrated him by forfeiting their matches. In return for this favor, Prince Edward has William released from the stocks and knights him, dubbing him Sir William. William returns to the tournament, defeats Count Adhemar, becomes the champion, and gets the girl. Because of the intervention of the handsome prince—who in this film is acting as the Fairy Godmother—it's safe to say William Thatcher lives happily ever after. Fairy tales sometimes come in strange shapes.

Another, more recent example is *The Blind Side*.

Sandra Bullock won an Oscar portraying the main character, a suburban Memphis mom who takes in Michael, a homeless black teenager. Michael starts the movie profoundly damaged—withdrawn, unloved, failing at school and at life.

By the end of the film, he has blossomed into a happy, academically successful, athletically gifted young man who goes on to college and pro football stardom. And Bullock won an Oscar for portraying his Fairy Godmother.

Note that having the word "Cinderella" in the title doesn't always make it a Cinderella story. *Cinderella Man*, starring Russell Crowe, tells the story of a Depression-era boxer who makes an incredible comeback and wins the heavyweight title.

The boxing is good, but the movie didn't do terribly well at the box office, taking in $61 million domestically on an estimated budget of $88 million. It seems that audiences expected a Cinderella story, but got a weak Monster story instead, with boxing opponent Max Baer standing in as the not-terribly-monstrous monster. Lesson: Movie titles can be important.

SHERLOCK HOLMES

The next Myth type we're going to explore is the detective or mystery story — the **Sherlock Holmes**.

It's exactly what it sounds like — the main character is confronted with a mystery that he seeks to solve. This is a common element of TV shows — nowadays called police procedurals — in which the audience follows each and every step the detective takes to solve a mystery.

What makes Sherlock Holmes a satisfying Myth story? We find mysteries threatening because they raise the question of whether the world can be managed by reason. By solving the mystery, the detective reasserts the primacy of reason, that all is well with the world. A perfect example of this symbolism is provided by the television series *NUMB3RS*, in which the mystery solving (which leads to criminal catching) is done by a super-rational professor of applied mathematics.

A couple of important points. First, by calling it Sherlock Holmes, I want to emphasize that it's not enough to have something that's a mystery for the audience. It has to be a mystery to the main character, who has to be trying to solve it.

A recent example of something mysterious that's not the right sort of mystery is in *Seven Pounds*. Will Smith plays Ben

Thomas, a character going around doing things the audience doesn't (and isn't supposed to) understand — spying on people, meeting with people, buying jellyfish. The audience may be wondering who he is and what he's doing, but there's no one onscreen aware of this mystery, trying to puzzle it out. And Ben, of course, knows exactly what he's up to, but he's not saying. In the end he commits suicide so he can give his internal organs to deserving people, to make up for causing an auto accident that killed his wife and several others.

So this isn't a Sherlock Holmes story, and its problem is that it isn't anything else either. In the end the movie is probably a Staying The Course story, but because everything's so mysterious, the audience doesn't know what Ben's problem is or how he's tempted to Devolve, so it doesn't really play.

The primacy of reason in Sherlock Holmes screenplays is often indicated by the main character, as in the case of the math professor in TV's *NUMB3RS*. This may be why films about psychics and mediums solving mysteries is a bit unsatisfying — having something not quite rational solve the mystery doesn't satisfy the underlying symbolism. On the other hand, in the TV show *Psych*, a hyper-observant detective solves mysteries while pretending to be a psychic, and in *The Mentalist*, a hyper-observant former fake psychic solves mysteries while making fun of those claiming to be psychics. These fit the Archetype just fine.

And it should be noted that Sherlock Holmes usually segues into Monster. Very seldom will solving a mystery be satisfying enough, in itself, to carry a screenplay. A very common example is a detective investigating a murder. He's probably not going to be satisfied simply to figure out who done it. Rather, that will lead to catching the killer—the monster—and either literally killing him or convicting him of the crime and thus metaphorically killing him. This is a very common pattern.

OZ

The next Myth type we're going to discuss is **Oz**. In this type of story, the main character is first shown living in his "normal" world. Then something happens to plunge him into an entirely different, completely unfamiliar world, with challenges unlike anything he's ever faced in the normal world. After dealing with those challenges, he ends up returning to the normal world.

The classic of this genre is, of course, *The Wizard of Oz*. A tornado picks up Dorothy (Judy Garland) in black-and-white Kansas and deposits her in Technicolor Oz, where upon landing she crushes the Wicked Witch of the East. Teaming up with the Scarecrow, the Tin Man, and the Cowardly Lion, she battles flying monkeys and travels through Oz, eventually killing the Wicked Witch of the West. She helps her companions, meets the Wizard, reveals him as a fraud, and finally returns home by clicking her heels together.

Oz is actually quite a common form of screenplay. Consider the well-known example of *Big*. Josh Baskin starts out as a short, suburban twelve-year-old who is magically transformed into a grown man (Tom Hanks). Finding he needs a job, he plunges into the adult world of nearby Manhattan, becoming an executive at a toy company, where he has to deal with the challenges of corporate politics and sexual interactions. Triumphant in that arena, he reverses the original magic, reverts to childhood, and returns to his home and his mom.

What are the common elements of this form, and why should it resonate with the audience?

Initially, the main character's life is out of balance, and he or she often expresses dissatisfaction with it, and, more than that, blames the situation on an external cause. Dorothy finds Kansas boring and daydreams and sings about how great life would be if she could get away and go "over the rainbow." Josh is disappointed that he is too short to go on an amusement park ride and wishes he could have a better life by being "big." Both unexpectedly have their wishes granted—Dorothy when she's transported to Oz, and Josh when he wakes up the next day fully grown.

Finding themselves in the new, strange world, the characters are disappointed to find they have not reached nirvana. They still face challenges, difficult challenges that they never would have encountered in their normal existence. They realize that having difficulties is not due to a problem in their environment, but is an inescapable part of the human condition. They also encounter other people who still have problems in this new world—Dorothy meets the Cowardly Lion, the Tin Man, and the Scarecrow, and Josh encounters Susan (Elizabeth Perkins), a fellow toy executive with her own life difficulties.

And while they tend to succeed in their strange-world endeavors—Dorothy kills the Wicked Witch and helps her companions Evolve; Josh impresses his boss in his job as a toy tester and gets pretty far with Susan—they realize that they desperately want to get back home.

They put huge effort into that, and succeed in returning to their normal worlds. The audience gets the feeling that their lives will improve as a result of their adventures: Dorothy expressly realizes that "there's no place like home," and we get the feeling that Josh will cope with his teen years better due to his experience with the adult world.

So why should Oz resonate so strongly with the movie audience? This form echoes the realization that there are no easy, external fixes to our problems.

Both Dorothy and Josh believe an external change would make their lives perfect. Dorothy wants to go over the rainbow, and Josh wants to be big. Both think that if their circumstances were different, their lives would be ideal.

Oz, therefore, is symbolic of our mistaken feeling that if something were different—if only we were older, or richer, or somewhere else—our lives would be idyllic.

A more recent example of the Oz Archetype is the popular comedy *The Hangover*. Four guys, including a groom-to-be, take off for a bachelor party in Las Vegas. It's not quite the same as *The Wizard of Oz* and *Big*: the guys don't want to live permanently in Vegas, but they think that if they can get to the city, the modern American version of Oz, a land where the normal rules of society don't apply, then they'll have a fabulous time beyond anything they could experience at home.

But like Dorothy and Josh, they find that things don't work out so trouble-free. Instead they find themselves dealing with endless difficulties, including amnesia, a tiger, Asian gangsters, and Mike Tyson. They lose the groom and have to find him before they can go back home. They put all their efforts into escaping Las Vegas, and eventually succeed. They go back to their normal world and lives (until the inevitable sequels, of course), and the audience suspects that they will live better as a result of their experiences.

Maybe the purest example of Oz is found in the late-'70s/ early-'80s television series *Fantasy Island*. Every week several guests would come from their humdrum existence to Mr. Roarke's island, convinced that they could experience great joy, at least temporarily, if they were only younger or better-looking or more famous. They get their wish, but things never work out the way they anticipated, and they Learn a Valuable Lesson—as TV characters are wont to do—before returning to their everyday lives.

Speaking of islands, let's look at a movie that has some, but not all, of the aspects of Oz: *Cast Away*. Chuck Noland (Tom Hanks again) plays a Federal Express efficiency expert whose life and job are totally ruled by the clock. He hitches a ride to Asia on a FedEx jet that goes off course and crashes in the Pacific. He washes ashore, the only survivor, and is stuck alone on a deserted island for four years.

So we have the most significant component of an Oz: a character goes from his normal world to a totally alien one. But what's missing is the asking—Chuck never says "I wish I didn't have to worry about that damn clock," or anything like that. In fact, he seems pretty happy and well-adjusted to his clock-dominated world. He and his fiancée (Helen Hunt) compare their calendars to try to figure out when they have time for each other, but neither complains about it.

The other thing off from classic Oz is that, while on the island, time difficulties have nothing to do with the emphasized difference. Remember, Josh's problems in *Big* stemmed from his lack of experience at being big. But the problems Chuck encounters in *Cast Away* certainly don't come from clocks not mattering—anyone used to modern society would have trouble surviving in the wilderness. So the story doesn't follow the same path — it's not about a character wishing for a change that suddenly presents him with new difficulties. Instead, it deals with a Job-like ability to survive and surmount problems.

Because not only does Chuck get shipwrecked, when he finally does get off the island and back to civilization, he's already had his funeral and his fiancée has married his endodontist. Chuck sums up the story by saying he's learned to keep on living despite his misfortunes.

So *Cast Away* doesn't have the request for an external change. It does have the transport to a strange world, the new problems there, and the thrilling escape back to the original world. Because it lacks the original request for change, it can't symbolically serve as a lesson that we can't avoid our inner flaws. It perhaps serves as a lesson that we can overcome anything life can throw at us, but it doesn't work the same way as the classic Oz.

SLEEPING BEAUTY

The final Myth Archetype is **Sleeping Beauty**. Its paradigm is provided by the fairy tale with the same name.

We all remember that story: a young, beautiful princess is cursed by an evil fairy, angry that she wasn't invited to the princess's christening. The princess pricks her finger on a poisoned needle and falls into an unwakeable sleep. There she remains for a hundred years, essentially dead, until a handsome prince finds her and kisses her, whereupon she comes back to life and lives happily ever after.

This is repeated, with the sexes reversed, in *Beauty and the Beast*. Beast started as a handsome prince, but was transformed into a hideous beast by an enchantress he insulted. He sits in his castle, dead to the world and human society.

Until Belle comes. At the end of the movie, after Beast is attacked and mortally wounded by the evil Gaston, Belle expresses her love for him just before he dies. This breaks the curse, bringing Beast back to life and transforming him back to handsome prince.

So that's the essence of the Sleeping Beauty story: a character is metaphorically dead because his or her life doesn't have any love in it. And that's what's needed to bring the character back to life — love.

Are there any examples in more adult movies? How about one of the most celebrated movies of all time, *Casablanca*. Humphrey Bogart's Rick Blaine is metaphorically dead at the top of the film, just going through the motions of life, carefully avoiding close relationships and political allegiances. Until lost love Ilsa Lund (Ingrid Bergman) walks into his bar, out of all the gin joints in the world. When Ilsa expresses her love for him, Rick comes back to life, just as Beast was brought back to life by Belle. He snaps out of his amorality, selflessly helps Ilsa's husband escape the Nazis, forces Ilsa to escape as well, and rededicates himself to fighting the bad guys.

Love has truly brought him back to life. That's the Sleeping Beauty Archetype, and it can really work for the audience.

QUEST

One more, though it's not really a Myth Archetype. But it's something that many screenwriters think of as a Myth Archetype: the **Quest**.

But Quest is not a real Myth form. It's simply when a character tries to do something. And as such, unless it's one of the true

Myth Archetypes outlined above, it's simply an Outer Game waiting for a Morph Archetype to be attached.

A man wants to get a Ph.D.? Outer Game. A girl wants to win a college scholarship? Outer Game. Sure, you can call these quests, but a screenplay's main character is almost always going to be trying to accomplish something. But unless it's a specific Myth Archetype, it will simply be an Outer Game, and unless the screenwriter supplies a Morph Inner Game, it's not going to hold the audience's interest.

◆ ◆ ◆

Those are the Myth Archetypes. Overall, think of it this way — if the Morph Inner Game is a screenplay's skeleton, then the Myth version is still a skeleton, but it's an exo-skeleton, like the one an insect has. It's on the outside, where you can see it, but it's still what gives the screenplay its shape and support. It stands in for the Morph skeleton.

MORPH/MYTH HYBRIDS

Now that we've introduced both Morph and Myth stories, note that the two types are often combined in a single screenplay. In the course of a Myth story, a character can simultaneously work on overcoming a character flaw, resulting in a Morph/Myth hybrid.

This is actually quite common, but the screenwriter has to take some care to keep the Morph and Myth stories compatible.

Gran Torino does it right. Clint Eastwood plays Walt Kowalski, an ornery widower who finds that his neighborhood has become heavily ethnic, affording him Hmong neighbors. Kowalski is withdrawn and unconnected, feeling nothing but annoyance toward both his nice neighbors and the Hmong gang that threatens them.

So Kowalski has to Evolve to the point where he can kill the monster. He has to learn to let down his guard, which allows him to get closer to his neighbors, especially the teenage boy who wants revenge when the gang rapes his sister. When Kowalski allows himself to care for them, then he's ready to put into action his plan to trick the gang into shooting him in front of witnesses so they'll go to jail and never threaten the neighborhood again. His Evolution leads quite logically to killing the Monster.

A more problematic fit is on display in *Philadelphia*. Tom Hanks won his first Best Actor Oscar for portraying Andrew Beckett, a lawyer who gets fired by his firm when he contracts AIDS and, in response, sues them with the help of lawyer Joe Miller (Denzel Washington).

It's not Beckett who Evolves in this story; it's Miller. Joe Miller is openly homophobic, and he doesn't much want to take Beckett's case. He has to Evolve in order to help his client do battle in court against the Monster of homophobia represented by the law firm. And that's a bit circular. Miller has to Evolve by overcoming his inner flaw of homophobia in order to kill the monster by bringing a lawsuit that is symbolic of overcoming homophobia. A little redundant. Better to follow the *Gran Torino* model, in which the character's Evolution equips him to kill a *different* monster.

MYTH COMBINATIONS

It's also possible to sometimes combine two Myth Archetypes. A wonderful example is the movie *Pretty Woman*, starring Julia Roberts and Richard Gere.

Ruthless businessman Edward Lewis (Gere) pays hooker-with-a-heart-of-gold Vivian Ward (Roberts) to stay with him for a week. Inevitably, they fall in love and end up together. Many have noted that Vivian's story is a Cinderella story, but it's fun to notice that Edward changes from emotionless financial killer to fully alive man in love in a classic Sleeping Beauty story. Cinderella meets Sleeping Beauty, and the result was a huge success.

◆ ◆ ◆

This part of the book has introduced the two types of Inner Game Archetypes. The next will go into more detail about how to actually construct them.

EXERCISE

Writing log lines for Myth screenplays is somewhat different. There aren't two Games, just the one. So the important thing is to clearly signal the Myth Archetype being used.

So, for example, for Monster one might write:

> A police chief, a shark hunter, and a scientist have a showdown with a giant, man-eating shark.

This immediately tells the audience it's a Monster story and gives them an idea of how difficult their task will be.

Write log lines for *Fatal Attraction*, *The Hangover*, and *Casablanca*.

Part Three
STRUCTURING YOUR SCREENPLAY, FOCUSING ON THE INNER GAME

Now we'll get down to more of the nuts-and-bolts of constructing your screenplay, making sure it has a strong Inner Game.

These are the chapters that will really help you get down to the real work.

CHAPTER SEVEN

WEAVING THE MORPH INNER AND OUTER GAMES

N WRITING A MORPH SCREENPLAY, it's vitally important to put into practice the theory expounded above; namely, that the Inner Game is the crucial component and, therefore, what the screenwriter must focus on. To repeat:

■ **A relentless focus on the Inner Game is what you need to make your screenplay succeed.**

Now this does not mean that the Outer Game is meaningless or irrelevant. It has several important *raisons d'être*.

First, it's probably what the screenwriter came up with first. After all, when you're trying to think of a movie premise, you're more likely to think "A guy finds a magical necktie" than "A guy has to learn to be less selfish" as your starting point.

And, of course, remember that the Outer Game serves the Inner Game, in two ways. First, it provides what the main character has to go through to overcome his inner flaw (in an Evolution story). And, equally important since you're writing a screenplay, the Outer Game affords the audience the opportunity to *see* the Inner Game take place. If a character's change from selfish to generous were purely internal, it wouldn't make much of a movie. The change has to be signaled to the audience, and, as the old saying goes, it's better to show than to tell.

So how do you come up with the Inner and Outer Games and make sure that they work together? First, some basic terminology will be useful. For years it's been customary to divide a screenplay into three acts, with Act II being twice the length of Acts I and III. So, in a 110-page script, there's a 27-page Act I, a 55-page Act II, and a 27-page Act III. These acts are what Aristotle more simply called the Beginning, Middle, and End.

As noted above, if you're sitting down to write a Morph screenplay, you're probably starting out with a general idea for your Outer Game. So now you have to come up with an idea for your Inner Game. Assuming you're writing an Evolution story (by far the most common type), try to think what kind of character flaw will fit in with your Outer Game. Think of how the Outer Game you've chosen could change a main character for the better, then set up the main character with that kind of flaw that he or she will overcome.

FIRST—ACT I, THE BEGINNING

Then focus on your Act I. First, how are you going to introduce your main character to illustrate his flaw? How is his emotional/psychological health less than perfect? This is the aspect of his personality that will finally improve, providing the audience a satisfying Evolution.

Sometimes the first time the audience meets the main character they're set up for the Evolution they're going to see. They want the main character to change, to overcome his flaw, and be a healthier version of himself.

An example of a screenplay that sets up its main character this way is *Hancock*, starring Will Smith. Hancock is introduced as a drunken, homeless, former superhero and his flaw is illustrated by a funny scene in which he tries to apprehend criminals but in the process destroys office buildings to the tune of millions of dollars. The audience nonetheless likes him because he's funny, he's quirky, and he's Will Smith. The movie effortlessly conjures in the audience's mind the hope that Hancock can Evolve, can change so as to overcome his problems and become the healthy superhero he was meant to be.

Sometimes it works differently. To go back to *Juno*, when we first meet the title character, we like her and don't necessarily hope that she'll change. But by the end of the movie, when we see how she has Evolved, we are happy for her and realize how much she needed it. Another example of a slow revelation of the inner flaw is in *Inception*. There, the main character's Outer Game plan of destroying a company is presented long before his flaw—he's unable to let go of his dead wife's memory—is revealed. The screenwriter has to decide when revealing his protagonist's flaw will be most effective.

In contrast, let's take a look at *Groundhog Day*, starring Bill Murray as Phil Connors, a man trapped in the same day, living it over and over endlessly. In the course of the movie, Phil Evolves from a snotty, sexist jerk to a genuinely caring man.

The problem is that at the top of the movie, Phil's jerk-ness doesn't really seem like a character flaw he can overcome; he just seems like a jerk. As a result, while this fine movie has excellent Acts II and III, the Inner Game takes an awfully long time to get going. Some in the audience may find Phil so unlikable that they give up before the Inner Game has a chance to fully kick in. But of course, if they hang in there, his Evolution is ultimately very satisfying.

Back to constructing our screenplay and continuing in Act I, the Outer Game begins with what is usually called the "inciting incident," an event that starts the main character along the course that will lead him to his Evolution. Once you've figured out what Outer Game you're going to use to change your main character, figure out how you're going to show the audience that story's beginning and include that in your Act I.

NEXT—ACT III, THE ENDING

After Act I, we turn not to Act II, but to Act III, the ending of the screenplay. In an Evolution story, this is when the main character completes his Evolution and becomes the healthier version of himself. Most movies have a decent Act III, because screenwriters generally know how their movies are going to end. Unless they're French movies.

Or unless they deliberately screw with it. Take *Duplicity*. Julia Roberts and Clive Owen play ex-spies who work an elaborate scheme to steal a commercial formula so they can sell it and make millions. The Inner Game is that they are both very guarded people who are attracted to each other, but can't quite bring themselves to trust each other.

After an elaborate con game, they acquire the formula and, as they wait to sell it, finally surrender themselves to both love and trust. Then the screenwriter twists everything—the commercial formula they've stolen is a fake. They've been played by one of the companies they thought they were stealing from, so they're not going to get their millions.

But the problem isn't in the Outer Game; it's that the Inner Game turns along with the Outer. When it turns out they're not getting their money, their love falls apart, too. One makes a sarcastic remark about at least still having each other, and the other joins in lamenting their situation. At the last moment, the audience has had the Inner Game chair pulled out from under them, and perhaps as a result the movie made just over $40 million domestically on an estimated budget of $60 million.

Getting back to constructing your screenplay, the Outer Game is completed in Act III as well. The relationship between the Outer and Inner Games is flexible: it might be that the main character has to complete his Evolution in order to achieve his goal in the Outer Game, or it might be that the main character has to abandon his Outer Game goal in order to complete his Evolution. But remember—the completion of the Inner Game is more important than achieving the goal of the Outer Game.

Turning again to *Hancock*, by the end of the movie John Hancock has indeed Evolved—he ends the film a confident superhero standing guard over New York City. He has overcome his flaws, his drunkenness, and his isolation. This movie has problems in Act II, but Acts I and III give the audience a satisfying experience. Hancock is set up as flawed in Act I and paid off as Evolved in Act III.

REALIZATION

A word about choosing an inner flaw—it's crucial that it be significant. If it's too small or inconsequential—the main character has to learn not to talk with his mouth full—the audience won't care that the character overcomes it.

Let's look at a concrete example, a type of story screenwriters sometimes attempt but which doesn't work and should definitely be avoided. I'll give this bad Archetype a name so you can remember it—I'll call it **Realization**. What it really is is a variation on producer Samuel Goldwyn's famous advice, "If you want to send a message, call Western Union." It most often comes up in highly politicized films, like the recent movies about American involvement in the wars in the Middle East.

The inadequate Inner Game in this type of movie is the idea that the main character's flaw is that he doesn't *realize* something that, fortunately, the screenwriter realizes and is happy to impart, to the main character and to the audience. The character overcomes his flaw by simply realizing this brilliant truth.

Tommy Lee Jones, in *In the Valley of Elah*, plays Hank Deerfield, a retired Army MP whose son has returned from duty in Iraq and apparently gone AWOL. Deerfield teams up with Emily Sanders (Charlize Theron), a police detective who finds that Jones' son has, in fact, been murdered and dismembered and his body burned. The two find a way to wrest jurisdiction away from the military and seek to discover who murdered the young soldier.

Although confronted with a series of false leads, they eventually discover the truth—Deerfield's son was killed by his own squad mates, apparently as a result of post-traumatic stress disorder. It is here, at the end of the film, that Deerfield has his Realization—that the Iraq War is uniquely bad in the history of the United States, if not the world, and that the U.S., as a result, is in terrible distress, which he signals by hanging a U.S. flag upside-down.

Deerfield doesn't really change at all, except that he no longer believes as much in the country and its military. He simply knows something new. Western Union, are you there?

Stay away from the Realization story.

It's also important that the Inner and Outer Games be compatible. In *Schindler's List*, Oskar Schindler Evolves from amoral to moral by helping Jews, so its association with the Holocaust is a good fit. On the other hand, consider the mismatch in *The Painted Veil*.

Edward Norton plays Walter Fane, a doctor trapped in a loveless marriage in 1920's Shanghai. When he discovers that his wife is having an affair, he vengefully volunteers to go to a remote Chinese village being ravaged by a deadly cholera epidemic, and forces her to go with him.

The Inner Game is clearly meant to be Evolution—will Fane overcome his desire to punish his wife for her infidelity? Will the resentful wife learn to appreciate her husband for the good man that he is?

The Outer Game affords them the opportunity, but it also overwhelms the Inner Game. The film has so many scenes of disease and terrible suffering, of dead bodies being carted from buildings, that the couple's marital woes, as Rick in *Casablanca* might say, don't amount to a hill of beans. The Outer and Inner Games are incompatible.

It's nice if the Inner Game and Outer Game are not just compatible, but mutually reinforcing. Take as an example *Fly Away Home*. The Outer Game is about a young girl using an ultra-light plane to lead a flock of geese on their migration home. The Inner Game is about her re-forming a relationship with her divorced father (going back home) after her mother is killed in an auto accident. The resonance between the two is quite satisfying.

A final point about Act III of a Morph screenplay—be careful not to end the Inner Game too soon. If you end the Inner Game, the audience probably isn't going to care about any Outer Game left to play out. I recently read a draft screenplay in which the main character finished his Evolution and still had a boxing match he wanted to win. The boxing match had nothing to do with the Inner Game, which was already over. So a good rule of thumb is to make the last scene in your screenplay the last scene in your Inner Game.

LAST—ACT II, THE MIDDLE

Having come up with the ideas for Acts I and II, we now turn to the hardest part of a screenplay, Act II. A lot of screenwriters get lost in Act II, in part because it's the longest act (approximately the length of Acts I and III combined).

It makes perfect sense to confront Act II last. Act II, after all, is really just how the main character is going to get from Act I to Act III. So you should know how Act III works out before you start in on Act II. If you start walking somewhere before you know where you want to go, chances are slim that you'll get to the right place.

But beyond that, the problems in Act II usually arise because the screenwriter loses focus on the Inner Game and instead concentrates on the Outer. He asks *What can happen?* instead of *How can I keep my main character Evolving?* And since anything can happen, it's hard to pick what should. In some comedies— *What Happens in Vegas*, for example—you'll find Act II laden with elaborate comedy pieces that unfortunately don't deal in any way with the characters' problems as they were set up in Act I.

Sometimes it's easy to keep focus on the Inner Game. Sometimes, indeed, the Outer Game *is* the Inner Game. Consider a couple of examples. In the HBO television show *In Treatment*, Gabriel Byrne plays a psychotherapist, and virtually every episode is entirely the therapist's session with a patient. The Inner and Outer Games are exactly the same—will the therapist be able to help his patient get better. The same thing is demonstrated in *Good Will Hunting*. The Outer Game is the same as the Inner: will Will Hunting (Matt Damon), with the help of his therapist (Robin Williams), overcome his past traumas and Evolve into the secure, adult genius he could be. By the way, *Good Will Hunting* is a great example of a screenplay that gives a supporting character his own Inner Game: Williams' character Evolves nearly as much as Damon's.

In other screenplays, aligning the two stories is easy because even though the Inner and Outer Games are not the same, they are clearly related. Let's look again at *Liar Liar*. Fletcher Reede is a habitually lying lawyer who (Inner Game) has to learn to be honest. The way that happens (Outer Game) is that a magic spell renders him incapable of lying. The Inner and Outer Games are so intimately related—he's going to learn to live honestly through being forced to live honestly—that they are naturally integrated. The experiences Reede goes through in the Outer Game naturally lead him to the Evolution inherent in the Inner Game.

The same is true for *Tootsie*. Michael Dorsey (Dustin Hoffman) learns to respect women through living as a woman. The Inner and Outer Games are meshed.

Integration doesn't always work out so easily, of course. If Rocky Balboa is fighting for the heavyweight boxing championship (Outer Game), but really has to learn that he's not the loser his father said he was (Inner Game), these are not so naturally related. It's still possible to make it work, but the screenwriter has to focus to avoid incoherence. If he gets distracted by the Outer Game, he can easily write some great boxing scenes that don't advance the Inner Game at all.

In Act II, the main character should be repeatedly getting either closer or farther away from his Evolution. Another way of looking at it is that the character in Act II should, like the stock market, be driven by *greed* and *fear*—greed for the goal of the Outer Game, and fear of the change required by the Inner Game. Why fear? Because change is difficult and scary. People usually have their character flaws, after all, as defense mechanisms, to keep themselves from getting hurt. That's why they fear giving them up. Or you can look at it another way—the audience has two fears: it shares the character's fear of change, but also fears for the character's fate if he doesn't change.

The journey through Act II should be difficult, but don't make the mistake of focusing on the Outer Game to make it difficult *physically*. That's okay, but the important thing is to focus on the Inner Game to make Act II difficult emotionally and psychologically.

If *Liar Liar* presents a well-integrated Act II, *Hancock* presents a poorly-integrated one. As outlined earlier, Act I sets up John Hancock as a drunk, homeless ex-superhero who accidentally destroys buildings when he tries to exert his powers and save the day. The audience wants him to find himself, overcome his alcoholism and homelessness, and be a superhero again.

The problem is, this is accomplished early in the movie. Public relations man Ray Embrey (Jason Bateman) convinces Hancock to enhance his image by going to prison voluntarily to pay his debt to society. Then he gets the police to let Hancock out so he can help with a bank hostage crisis. Hancock ends the standoff, freeing the hostages and capturing the bad guys, and the movie seems prematurely over partway through Act II. Hancock's Evolution already seems complete.

Then the screenplay's curveball—it turns out Hancock, who has amnesia, was in the past hooked up with Mary Embrey (Charlize Theron), who is now Ray's wife and herself a secret, nonpracticing superhero. Suddenly the movie veers off onto a whole new Inner Game—is Hancock going to get back together with Mary, or is he going to break it off and leave her to Ray, at least until Ray grows old and the eternally young Mary is looking for a new life partner? And to get this thread going, the screenplay has to introduce something hard to follow about how Hancock and Mary are no longer invulnerable when they get too close together.

So that's the big problem with Act II—the screenplay sets up one Inner Game and then in Act II tries to change to another one. It didn't work, but at least the filmmakers made the right choice and ended the movie by essentially going back to the original Inner Game and repeating the beat showing John Hancock Evolved, cured of his original flaw.

So the lesson for the screenwriter is, stick with the Inner Game you set up in Act I and pay off in Act III as you make your way through Act II. It's okay to veer off the Inner Game for some great action or comedy, but remember that the Inner Game functions as the spine of the script—the other material has to hang off it.

Let's summarize how the Inner and Outer Games are woven together to create the Morph script.

Act I

- Set up the main character and inner flaw of the Inner Game.

- Start the Outer Game with the inciting incident, moving into Act II.

Act III

- Complete the main character's Outer Game in some way, whether by achieving it, abandoning it, etc.

- Finish the main character's Evolution (or, of course, his Devolution or Staying The Course) to complete the Inner Game.

- Make sure there's no significant action that comes after the Inner Game has been completed.

Act II

- Engage the main character in his Inner Game journey, from flawed in Act I to Evolved in Act III.

- Let the main character try to achieve his goal in the Outer Game and either make progress or lose ground.

◆ ◆ ◆

That's the basic approach to formulating and meshing a Morph screenplay's Inner and Outer Games. The next chapter will deal with the same process in the case of a Myth screenplay.

EXERCISE

Here's a great tool to use when you're structuring your Morph screenplay—the **Inner/Outer Game Outline**.

Take four sheets of paper to represent the screenplay. Page 1 will be Act I, pages 2 and 3 will be the first and second halves of Act II (call them Act IIA and Act IIB), and page 4 will be Act III.

Divide the pages in half vertically and label the left side "Outer Game" and the right side "Inner Game." The first page will look something like this:

ACT I

OUTER GAME	INNER GAME

Fill in the beats of the Inner and Outer Games in the proper Acts, in the blank spaces.

When you start plotting out your screenplay, this format will help you keep your Inner and Outer Games aligned.

You're done when both the Inner and Outer Games are filled in and consistent with one another. Read through each separately to make sure they both make sense, then read them together to make sure they don't conflict in any way. This will help you have a fully fleshed-out and satisfying outline on which to base your Morph screenplay.

Screen *The Queen*, and fill out the Inner/Outer Game Outline as you watch.

CHAPTER EIGHT

CONSTRUCTING THE MYTH STORY

THE MYTH SCREENPLAY works differently from the Morph. In the Morph screenplay, there are distinct Inner and Outer Games, and the main danger the screenwriter has to avoid is concentrating on the less-important Outer Game instead of the more-important Inner.

In the Myth story, remember, the Inner and Outer Games are not distinct. Instead, the Outer Game—for example, killing a monster—is symbolic of the Inner Game. The monster symbolizes the flaw being overcome. As a result, there's no need for a separate Inner Game. When police chief Martin Brody (Roy Scheider) goes out in a boat to kill the shark in *Jaws*, we don't get to see him work through an inner problem. We don't have to—when he kills the shark, he is symbolically killing his (or humanity's) inner flaw.

So the screenwriter only has to write the Outer Game, and the Inner Game takes care of itself. Now that may sound like an

exception that swallows the whole rule—you may be thinking, I
don't have to learn anything about this Inner Game stuff so long
as I write a Myth screenplay. Problem solved.

Well, it's not that simple. In a Myth story, it's important that
the Outer Game be properly constructed, so that it does, in fact,
have the intended symbolic effect.

Let's take a Monster story as an example of how to construct
a Myth screenplay. The steps are roughly analogous to those in
constructing a Morph Story. We attack the Acts in the same
order: Act I, Act III, Act II.

FIRST—ACT I, THE BEGINNING

First, in Act I, the screenwriter introduces the monster. It need not
be superpowerful at this point—that can come later. But at some
point in Act I the monster starts threatening the main character
and, ideally, other innocent people. Maybe even the whole world.
The more threatening, the more monstrous.

NEXT—ACT III, THE ENDING

Now look to Act III. How is the main character going to finally
defeat the monster? This usually involves the main character's
having an insight that the monster—otherwise seemingly
undefeatable—cannot match. The shark in *Jaws* doesn't know that
it's not a good idea to chomp on a tank of compressed air, while
Chief Brody realizes it's a fine idea to shoot the tank with a rifle
to make it explode in the shark's mouth.

Note that it usually works best if the main character is the
one who actually kills the monster. The screenwriter changes
that at his peril. For example, in *Edge of Darkness*, Mel Gibson

plays Thomas Craven, a Boston detective whose daughter is murdered in front of him. Craven Solves The Mystery, figuring out why his daughter was murdered, and he partially Kills The Monster by gunning down several of the men involved, but it's left to another character, Darius Jedburgh (Ray Winstone), to finish the Monster killing by shooting the last few bad guys. This is presented as a sort of Evolution story for Jedburgh, but it ultimately would have been more satisfying to see Craven eliminate all the bad guys. Again, the issue is symbolism: since Monster is symbolic of overcoming an inner flaw, it makes little sense for a third party to fortuitously do some of the killing.

FINALLY — ACT II

Then we turn to what is again the hardest part — Act II. In a Monster screenplay, it's essentially writing an Outer Game about battling the monster, but the smart screenwriter will keep in mind when structuring it that it symbolizes the Inner Game. So he will have the main character struggle against the monster, sometimes gaining a little and sometimes losing a little. Just as it looks like he can't possibly win, he has the insight that allows his victory.

In the next section, we'll look at special screenwriting situations: adaptations, sequels, and remakes.

EXERCISE

Here's a version of the tool we used to structure your Morph screenplay, but revised to help in structuring a Myth screenplay — the **Outer Game/Symbolic Meaning Outline**.

Again, take four sheets of paper to represent the screenplay. Divide the pages in half vertically, and this time label the left

side "Outer Game" and the right side "Symbolic Meaning." The
first page will look
something like this:

With a Myth screenplay, you'll fill the left side with beats for the
Outer Game and the right side with the symbolic meaning of those
beats.

Again, when you're done, read through the columns separately to
make sure they both make sense, then read them together to make
sure they align properly. This will help you have a fully fleshed-out
and satisfying outline on which to base your Myth screenplay.

EXERCISE

Screen *Fatal Attraction* and *The Hangover*, and fill in an Outer
Game/Symbolic Meaning Outline for each as you watch.

Part Four
ADAPTATIONS, SEQUELS, AND REMAKES

Screenwriters often develop screenplays based on other material, like books or previous movies. This part of the book will deal with some of those situations from the Inner Game point of view.

CHAPTER NINE

ADAPTATIONS

ADAPTING A NOVEL, play, comic book, or true story poses special problems for the screenwriter. They stem from the fact that these other forms are exactly that — other. They're different from movies. The screenwriter has to be careful not to mistake the quality of the original material for quality of the adapted screenplay.

Take a novel, for example. Obviously, reading a novel and watching a movie are very different experiences. The average novel contains around 100,000 words; the average screenplay only 20,000. We can read a few pages of a novel, reread a paragraph, put the book down to think about it. Pick the book back up, reread the last page, read the next fifty pages, and so on. A clever word choice or turn of phrase can catch our attention.

The nooks and crannies of a book are important and can make the book a good one, even if there's not much of a unifying story. Indeed, to many modern readers, the sentence-by-sentence writing of a novel is the important thing, while story is superfluous and old-fashioned.

Movies are different. For most people, watching a film is an immediate, immersive experience. When we're in the theater we can't stop the film to think about it. We can't, usually, hear a character's thoughts or see that another character reminds her of long-gone Aunt Sophie.

So we have to go back to the original thesis of this book—what matters in a screenplay is the Inner Game. That holds true whenever we try to write a screenplay, even if it's an adaptation of a novel that may itself not have much of an Inner Game. And it holds true equally for adaptations of plays, songs, posters, news articles, whatever.

■ **If your source material doesn't have an Inner Game, you have to come up with one, or your screenplay will be flat and unsatisfying.**

I recently consulted with a screenwriter who was hired to adapt a nonfiction book into a feature screenplay. The book covered recent historic events in Washington, and, as nonfiction, succeeded. Many readers are fascinated by what goes on behind the scenes at the highest levels of government. Finding out the truth is what nonfiction books are about. Same for documentaries.

But not feature films. That's simply not why most people go to see them.

When I read his first draft, I said, there's no story—meaning there's no Inner Game. The screenplay competently laid out the series of events, choosing the most significant from the book, and dramatized them nicely.

But it didn't concentrate on any one character to show that character's Evolution or Devolution. It didn't have what a feature audience wants. The nonfiction book was interesting on its own terms, revealing behind-the-scenes events that shaped history. And the topic would probably make a fascinating documentary. But as a feature, it was hollow and unsatisfying.

Let's take a look at a produced film with a similar problem. *Changeling*, based on a true story, stars Angelina Jolie as Christine Collins, a single mother in 1928 whose young son is missing when she comes home from work. She is understandably frantic, making her own calls while the police search for the boy.

Finally, five months after the disappearance, the police find the boy—who says he's been kidnapped—and return him to his mother. But she has a problem—the boy doesn't look to her like her son. The police explain that away, but Christine isn't completely convinced, especially since the boy is now three inches shorter than he was before he was taken.

When she raises these issues, the authorities respond by throwing her into an insane asylum until she can prove she's sane by—you guessed it—admitting that the returned boy is in fact her son. The movie depicts this as a surprisingly common way of dealing with difficult women who, if they continue to fight, are also subjected to electroshock treatments.

Aided by a sympathetic preacher, Christine gets out of the asylum and brings a lawsuit against the city, as a result of which all the women wrongfully confined are released and the city has to find another way to deal with difficult Ovarian-Americans.

We'll get back to the son in a second. The point here is that Christine certainly goes through a lot, but, unfortunately, it doesn't add up to Evolution. At the end of the process she's a bit more assertive and less polite than she was at the beginning, but she doesn't really start out with a flaw that she overcomes as a result of going through this extraordinary and horrific series of events. In fact, at the beginning she's portrayed as an entirely competent woman and loving mom. Audiences like to see characters change significantly, so it's usually a mistake to start a character off too good. The unfortunate result is that *Changeling*, on the Morph front, is missing an Inner Game.

The movie attempts to become Myth at some point, by focusing on the investigation that ends up finding and capturing the monster who, in fact, took and murdered the son and a number of other boys. Unfortunately, Christine's character wasn't a police officer, so the Monster story focuses on another character entirely, the detective pursuing the murderer. This story actually works pretty well, but a movie can't succeed when it has such a bifurcated structure.

Since this was an adaptation of a true story, the screenwriter can protest that that's the way it was in real life. But that's not a good excuse. When you're writing any screenplay, even an adaptation, it's got to follow the Inner Game rules if it's going to be effective and entertaining. The audience wants to be entertained — they're not going to leave the theater saying "I'm quite satisfied, because that would have been really good if only the source material had been better."

Contrast *Changeling* with the highly successful *Erin Brockovich*. Also based on a true story, that film's Outer Game involves the attempt to bring a utility company to justice and get them to clean up the environmental damage they've caused through their careless handling of toxins.

But it was the Inner Game that brought the film to life and handed star Julia Roberts an Oscar. The Outer Game was just there to give the Inner Game a chance to play out.

Here's the first sentence of *Variety*'s review of the film:

> An exhilarating tale about a woman discovering her full
> potential and running with it, *Erin Brockovich* is everything that
> "inspirational" true-life stories should be and rarely are.

They knew it was the Inner Game that was going to make this movie a hit. And later in the review, raving about Roberts' performance:

> As for Roberts, she has never been more winning, bringing the full force of her dazzling personality to bear on a character well on her way to being a total loser, but who resolutely refuses to go that route.

This Evolution is the meat of the screenplay. All the rest of it—the contaminated residents, the gruff boss, the low-cut blouses—add flavor and help the movie win audiences over. No one's saying that having a good Inner Game is all you need. It's not sufficient, but it's necessary. Whether the screenplay is an adaptation or springs completely from the writer's head, it's absolutely necessary. And *Erin Brockovich* wisely focused on exactly that aspect, and succeeded because of it.

Getting back to the adaptation of the nonfiction book, when I told the writer that his screenplay lacked an Inner Game, sure enough he defended himself by saying that the book didn't have one, that it was just reportage. When I said that he had to insert one, even if it wasn't in the book, he said he didn't think he was allowed to deviate that much from the source material.

If he'd told me that before he started, I guess the only advice I could have given him would have been to pass on the project, unless what he really cared about was the writing fee, of course.

Because when the producers do get around to reading your Inner Game-free script, they're not going to like it and it isn't going to move forward. So if the project is stacked against you that way, don't waste your time.

Of course, it's worth pointing out that adapting a true story may have a special difficulty: changing a true story to augment the Inner Game can seem unfair to the real people involved. Maybe the story would be better if a certain character were secretly an alcoholic, but if he actually wasn't an alcoholic, it might even be defamatory to write the screenplay that way. That's a problem that anyone writing such an adaptation has to deal with. Consider this from a *Washington Post* editorial on the film *Fair Game*, based on the true story of exposed CIA agent Valerie Plame and her husband, diplomat Joe Wilson:

> *Fair Game* . . . is full of distortions — not to mention outright inventions . . . . Hollywood has a habit of making movies about historical events without regard for the truth; *Fair Game* is just one more example.

So when you're adapting a true story, you have to be careful. In the next chapter, we move on to sequels.

EXERCISE

Screen *My Sister's Keeper*. This adaptation of a novel was quite controversial in that it changed a significant event in the Outer Game. This riled the book's fans, but would have been worth it if it had improved the Inner Game.

After you've watched the movie, ask yourself whether the change (if you don't know what changed, you can look it up on the Internet) in fact improved the Inner Game. (I don't think it did, so while I applaud the producers for having the courage to make the change, I wonder exactly why they thought it would improve the final product.)

CHAPTER TEN

SEQUELS

NOWADAYS, IT SEEMS any movie that makes big money will eventually spawn a sequel. After all, the thinking goes, the concept's presold. People flocked to *Linoleum*, so they'll surely go see *Linoleum 2*. We'll just sit back and rake in the money.

So what's the problem? The problem is, if the original movie did well, it's because it had an audience-pleasing Inner Game, which ended when the movie did. We can bring back the star, the director, and the cute dog, but unless we can come up with an Inner Game that's as compelling as the original's, it's not going to work as well.

There are several possible strategies for coming up with a new Inner Game:

- Put the main character into the same basic situation while rewinding his character back to its original, flawed state.

- Have the main character overcome a whole new flaw.

- Have the main character confront and try to kill a whole new monster.

- Switch from Morph to Myth, or vice versa.

The dangers are numerous. An obvious one is that the sequel can be too similar to the original. The audience may feel ripped off, that they've simply been tricked into watching, and paying for, the same movie they saw the first time. Another is that the same Inner Game simply won't be as good the second time around.

Let's take a look at some examples of the sequel process. The original *Die Hard*, starring Bruce Willis as New York detective John McClane, was a big box office hit. It combined a Morph Evolution story—McClane has to learn his wife's value, and she his—with a Monster story—McClane has to stop terrorists who have seized his wife and her coworkers in an elaborate scheme to steal millions of dollars in bonds. Both the Evolution and the Monster elements were handled well and worked beautifully.

By the end of the film, McClane has overcome his flaw (as has his wife and a police officer who had tragically lost the nerve to shoot suspects), and the bad guys have been stopped and killed. So when the studio calls and says they want a sequel, what's a screenwriter to do?

Basically, *Die Hard 2* takes the route of ignoring the original's Morph story and going completely with a Monster storyline. McClane starts out having worked things out with his wife, indeed he's at the airport to pick her up. That's where he encounters the new monster: a renegade military group that plans to rescue a Latin American dictator from American custody and as a strategy is screwing up the country's air traffic control system and crashing airliners.

How'd the sequel do? It did fine, outgrossing the original, although it also cost considerably more to make. It certainly lacked the Morph component of the original, but made up for it, at least with some segment of the audience, in bigger action sequences.

But wait! There have been two more sequels in the *Die Hard* franchise. The third film in the series, *Die Hard: With a Vengeance*, added Samuel L. Jackson and Jeremy Irons, but little Inner Game. Once again, it didn't have much of a Morph story, concentrating on Monster. This one was generally considered a disappointment, both creatively and financially—it cost even more than the first sequel, while grossing a little less.

The most interesting thing about the final (or at least most recent) sequel, *Live Free or Die Hard*, is that the producers wisely went full circle, back to the Evolution Inner Game of the original. Or close.

In the original, the marriage of McClane and his wife is on the rocks, with him resenting her career, with the Evolution story ultimately resulting in his learning to value her and give her some freedom, and her simultaneously learning to value him as a man and protector.

Well, McClane's wife left him around the second sequel, so she's not around for the third. But there is his estranged daughter, who—like her mother in the original—has dropped the McClane surname in favor of mom's maiden name.

So, as McClane and a young sidekick kill the Monster by trying to stop a hacker who is attacking the nation's cyberstructure in an extremely convoluted scheme to make a lot of money, he's really on the Inner Game path to reconciling with his daughter.

The ending of *Live Free or Die Hard* feels eerily close to the original's. This time, McClane has discovered his daughter's good qualities—she's not the complete pain he thought she was—and she has discovered his. In fact, like her mother before her, she abandons mom's maiden name and calls herself by dad's last name, at least for the day. And the movie did pretty well, grossing more than $380 million worldwide, making it the highest grossing of the four *Die Hard* movies. Going back to the old Inner Game worked, and probably few, if any, in the audience consciously noted the parallel.

And consider *Rocky*. In the original film, a run-down club fighter, Rocky Balboa (Sylvester Stallone), gets the opportunity to fight for the boxing heavyweight title. As noted earlier, his opponent Apollo Creed is a loudmouth, but no monster, and the Inner Game is Evolution: Rocky has to learn that he's not a loser. He's beaten in the championship bout, but successfully Evolves from his original state.

After Rocky wins the championship belt in *Rocky II*, the series switches gears to Monster stories in *Rocky III*, *Rocky IV*, and *Rocky V*, before switching back to an Evolution story in the well-received fifth sequel, *Rocky Balboa*.

So, once again, the lesson is that the screenwriter doing a sequel must follow the Inner Game rule just as if he were writing a completely original movie. The screenplay needs a compelling Inner Game, so either characters must Evolve or Monsters must be Killed (or one of the other Archetypes, but these are by far the most common). The sequel has some built-in marketing advantages, but no built-in story advantages — that's still up to the screenwriter.

The next chapter will conclude the special situations by taking a look at remakes.

CHAPTER ELEVEN

REMAKES

THE LAST SPECIAL CASE we'll deal with is the remake. If it makes sense to do a sequel to a successful movie, how much more sense does it make to redo it altogether? Isn't there a built-in audience? They liked it the first time, right?

Although, to be fair, the idea isn't usually to get the same audience to stop by again. Rather, it's to go for a new audience that missed the movie the first time and isn't inclined to find it now. Maybe the stars are no longer current or maybe it was made in 2D. But the movie worked, so all we should have to do is "update it." New stars, new director, and it'll all be good.

But what about the script? Seldom is the same script reused. Generally a lot more is done than just changing "Roosevelt" to "Obama" and "World War II" to "the war in Afghanistan." Actors don't want to get criticized for doing a carbon copy and screenwriters want to do their own thing.

So we're left with the same problem that screenwriters generally have—coming up with a script with a compelling Inner Game that will involve the audience. As with an adaptation, this difficulty is sometimes increased by the calls for fidelity to the original. And as we said before, fidelity should be your last concern; a good Inner Game should be your first.

Let's take a look at a couple of examples. First, *Invasion of the Body Snatchers*. The original—itself an adaptation of a novel—was made in 1956. It is a Monster story: a small-town doctor finds that his neighbors are turning into emotionless shells of their former selves. He eventually discovers that alien plant pods are duplicating people in preparation to dominate the world, and he, of course, may be the only one able to stop them.

Made during the "Red Scare" era of the 1950s, the movie's zombie-manufacturing Monster is often said to represent either Communism, or, conversely, the spread of Commie-hating, fear-mongering McCarthyism. The protagonist must first figure out what's transforming people, then fight back and try to stop what's happening. In the end, he successfully alerts the authorities and we're led to believe that the aliens will be dealt with and defeated. Our hero has helped to Kill The Monster.

A remake was made in 1978 with the same title, starring Donald Sutherland and Brooke Adams. It's essentially the same Monster story, with zombie-like pod people popping up every-where and threatening the survival of humanity. Of course, any Cold War allusions are long gone, with critics instead now seeing the aliens as representing the media-obsessed, consumerist threat of the new version's era.

There is, however, one huge difference between the two versions. In the original, the hero successfully kills the Monster by alerting the authorities to the aliens' presence and plans. The remake ends more bleakly—our hero becomes a pod person. The Monster kills us. If the original is Mythically analogous to an Evolution story, the remake is analogous to a Devolution story.

Aside from the ending, from an Inner Game point of view the remake follows the contours of the original pretty closely. And because of that, both versions work, and were each successful and well-regarded upon release.

Which is not the case for the next example: *The Heartbreak Kid*. In the original 1972 dark comedy hit, Charles Grodin plays Lenny Cantrow, a man who's on his honeymoon when he meets gorgeous Kelly Corcoran (Cybill Shepherd) and immediately loses all interest in his new wife.

The Heartbreak Kid is a Devolution story. Lenny starts out relatively healthy, but quickly turns on his new wife. To be fair, she is annoying, with an irritating laugh and a repulsive way of eating egg salad, but we are led to assume that Lenny had a pretty good idea what she was like before he said "I do." So we don't give him much sympathy when he decides she's suddenly not the one for him, and heartlessly dumps her for the fantasy girl he's just met.

Throughout the movie Lenny's behavior becomes worse and worse, Devolving before our eyes. Our only hope for him, in a strange way, is that Kelly seems sure to reject him and bring him to his senses. Instead, implausibly, Kelly agrees to marry him.

Which gives us the movie's kicker—at the Lenny-Kelly wedding reception, Lenny seems unhappy with where he's ended up. Having sold his soul to the devil, he doesn't even get to enjoy the run-up to hell.

All in all, the original Devolution tale works brilliantly.

The remake goes in a very different direction. Made in 2007, it stars Ben Stiller in the Charles Grodin role, and it utterly rejects the Devolution story. The main difference is that while Lenny must have known what his new wife was like, Stiller's "Eddie" Cantrow has no idea. The audience is right along with him when he meets and courts the new wife, who seems to all of us to be pretty much perfect.

It's not until they're on their way to the honeymoon that Eddie—along with the audience—learns the truth: his new bride is a sadomasochistic, unemployed, coke-snorting nutjob. Eddie becomes as deceptive and sneaky as Lenny, but his new wife is so horrible that when he meets the Other Woman, there's absolutely no doubt that he'd be doing the right thing to dump Miss Wrong.

Unfortunately, the Devolution of the original film isn't replaced by anything. The situation is played for laughs, but there's no depth of character. The result is a movie with an Outer Game but no Inner Game. And it showed in the box office results—the domestic gross barely topped $36 million.

Could the sequel have worked? Only if the screenwriter had come up with some kind of Inner Game. The general rule bears repeating yet again:

■ **A relentless focus on the Inner Game is the key to writing a successful screenplay.**

So the key to writing a remake is just the same old key—Inner Game. It's complicated by the existence of the original, but to do a good job, you've got to overcome it.

◆ ◆ ◆

The next part of the book will deal with writing not for the big screen, but for the little one—television.

EXERCISE

Think of one of your favorite older movies. If you were asked to rewrite it, how would you change the story? Pay particular attention to the Inner Game of the original and how it might be modified.

Part Five
WRITING FOR TELEVISION

Up to this point, the book has dealt mainly with feature writing. The same considerations apply when writing for television, although with variations.

CHAPTER TWELVE

TELEVISION—MORPH, MYTH, AND HYBRID

N
OW WE'LL TURN TO THAT STEPSISTER of feature films, television. How, if at all, does the Inner Game of Screenwriting apply?

First question: What's the difference between the two forms?—an issue that is often misunderstood. The typical response would be length; that features are about two hours long while TV episodes are only thirty or sixty minutes. But that's the wrong comparison, because what we ought to be comparing to feature films are not television *episodes*, but television *series*, which can be 100 hours long, or even longer.

A TV series can be thought of as a slow-motion feature, with an endless Act II, that will go on and on, week by week, for a hundred episodes or more (if the producers are lucky). The pilot contains a very brief Act I, setting up the situation and characters, then moves on to the first sequence of Act II. Later episodes pile on more Act II, and, if the showrunners know that the series is going to end, they can tack on a brief Act III at the end. It's in the series as a whole that a television creator will seek to insert a compelling Inner Game. And—once again—it's this Inner Game that makes for a successful effort.

Let's look at a couple of well-constructed series to see how it's done.

First, *The Sopranos.* We all know about the brilliant dialog and acting. But it's the overall setup that gave the show its long life and success. Tony Soprano is totally concerned with power: he craves power over others, and his greatest fear is that others will gain power over him. In his eyes, it's a kill-or-be-killed world, and he fully intends to be the killer.

On the other hand, he's a charming, funny guy. If I weren't terrified of him, I'd love to be his buddy and hang out with him. He can be great to his friends, his wife, his children.

So there's a TV series' basic setup—the main character has an inner flaw (Tony is a murderous thug), but is likeable enough that the audience is going to watch the show to see if he can eventually overcome the flaw, Evolve. From week to week, he gets a little healthier or less healthy, and the audience goes right along with him. This is especially true in Tony's case, because he's caught in a dilemma—if he gets too nice, he'll be vulnerable to being killed on the job, and if he gets too nasty, he risks alienating his family and dying alone.

That's the basic formula for a Morph show. Want another example? How about *House?* Main character Gregory House is an absolutely brilliant medical diagnostician with a flaw—he dislikes pretty much everybody, including his underlings and patients— and can't form real relationships with anyone. We like House—

because he's brilliant and he's funny—and hope from week to week that he will make progress in overcoming this problem. The show also tries to set up a *Sopranos*-like dilemma: House, at least, believes that if he changes too much, becomes too nice, he'll lose his abilities in the medical arena.

So, to reiterate, the typical Morph TV series is a long, slow story with the potential for Evolution or Devolution in the long run.

What about Myth shows? Plenty of those around. The most obvious examples are what people in the TV business call "police procedurals," usually examples of Monster or Sherlock Holmes.

Take as an example the long-lived *Law & Order*. The detectives and prosecutors each week solve a mystery, catching and prosecuting a murderer, thus killing a monster who threatens society. (It's interesting to note the difference between old shows like *Adam 12* and modern cop shows like *Criminal Minds*—I guess back in the '50s and '60s *any* crime was enough to bother us; now it takes a serial killer to get our juices flowing.)

Indeed, many television shows are episodic examples of pure Myth Archetypes. Police procedurals are weekly Sherlock Holmes and Monster stories. *Fantasy Island* was almost always an Oz. It's a good way to construct a series.

Most shows nowadays are hybrids, combinations of both Morph and Myth elements. The big question is the proportions of the two types. *House*, for example, has elements of Myth—every week the brilliant doctor tries to kill the monstrous disease that threatens his patient. But the real focus of each episode is on the character of House. He always solves the mystery of what's killing his patient, and usually saves the patient's life, but the focus of the show is on House's flaw and whether he's going to get better or worse that week. In *Law & Order*, by contrast, the Mythic mystery and prosecution dominate the show. Morph elements are there, but in the typical episode they play a much smaller part. But they're important in setting the tone of the series.

In *Law & Order*, longtime assistant DA Jack McCoy is mainly concerned with right and wrong. Obviously that motivates him to prosecute the killers, but it also provides moments where he can wonder if what he is doing is right: should he pressure a defendant by threatening his wife, for example. But where *House* is 80% Morph, 20% Myth, *Law & Order* has those proportions reversed.

Having a show be mainly Myth is quite typical of procedurals. They tend to be mainly about that week's case, with the cops' character flaws thrown in for flavor. An interesting lesson is contained in *CSI: Crime Scene Investigation*. Back in *CSI*'s pilot and early episodes, every character had a prominent backstory, and every pair of characters had a complex, often contentious, relationship.

But as the show went on and became a hit, the creators realized that the audience was fascinated by the cases, not the characters' peccadilloes. The team members became more about running mass spectrometers and less about their gambling problems or internecine warfare. The show, in other words, became noticeably more Myth and less Morph.

Primarily Myth shows like *Law & Order* generally get their Morph elements through guest characters who go through a Morph Inner Game. That, by the way, is why so many TV shows involve cops, lawyers, or doctors: although these characters may not be going through a particularly dramatic life moment, the civilians they're dealing with are very likely going through some of the most stressful and dramatic situations of their lives. When a wife decides to testify against her husband or a son has to pull the plug on his father, it's a highly dramatic moment.

And a quick note to show that Myth procedurals need not always be police shows. *The West Wing*, set in the White House, was really a non-police procedural. The characters were somewhat flawed, but the typical episode wasn't about whether they were going to get better. The typical episode was instead about whether some evil party—generally Republicans or other conservatives—would be defeated. The pilot, for example, climaxes when Christian fundamentalists are stopped from having assistant chief of staff Josh Lyman fired for something he said during a televised interview. Josh learns something in the episode—not to say bad things on TV about Christian fundamentalists—but the focus is on defeating the threat to him and the Bartlett Administration. In other words: Monster.

And one other observation: because a TV series is so long, in a Monster series, the qualities used to kill the monster can be emphasized and can make the series distinctive.

In a Monster feature, the screenplay is so short that the characters will generally use the usual, expected personal qualities in trying to kill the monster: bravery, persistence, innovation, etc. But in a TV series, a particular set of qualities can be used. In *The West Wing*, for example, the characters use "progressive" ideas in their attempts to defeat their rivals.

Or consider *The Unit*. In that series, members of a secret U.S. Special Forces team fight week after week to defeat foreign militaries and terrorists who threaten the country. With what qualities? With stoic masculinity and military honor, which the episodes always emphasize. It's this emphasis that gave the series its distinctive flavor and made it different from other series in that same arena.

In *Columbo*, the main character solves crimes not solely with brilliant observation and deduction, but also with his ever-present regular-guyness. Most of the criminals he confronts and catches are rich and/or holders of highly prestigious positions, and Lt. Columbo is far below them in social standing. The unspoken message is that common sense can solve the problems created by those of high rank.

What about situation comedies? They follow the same rules, and they tend to be Morph shows. The main character has a flaw, a comic flaw, a flaw that makes him or her look silly. In each episode an Outer Game is introduced that highlights the flaw, the difficulties it creates for the character, and the costs it imposes on the character and his family or friends. The character wrestles with his or her flaw, ultimately resolving the situation but failing to get over the flaw. Everyone has a good laugh, and everything goes back to normal so we can do it all again the next week.

This is true of sitcoms, up to and including the most prestigious and recognized—like *Seinfeld*. That series is famously said to be about nothing, but it's not: it's about characters whose lives are about nothing. The characters have nothing significant in their lives which are, as a result, comically empty. That's their shared flaw, and exaggerating it is the source of the show's comedy. What, after all, is the episode in which Jerry can't remember the name of the woman he's dating ("The Junior Mint") besides an exaggerated view of our hookup culture? So the Inner Game theory applies perfectly.

Every TV series starts with a pilot. Writing a television pilot is one of the most difficult writing tasks there is. Think about it: the writer has to set up the characters and the situation, yet still tell a compelling story, and all in the standard length of only 22 or 44 minutes (not counting commercials). Just telling a story in that length of time is difficult enough! And by the way, judging a potential series based on just the pilot is also very difficult, analogous to judging a feature screenplay based on the first page or two. After all, an hour-long pilot might seem great on first viewing, but really just be the great first hour of a two-hour feature, unable to carry the weight of a hundred episodes. So maybe we should all have a bit more sympathy for television executives.

Each episode of a series is a sequence in an endless Act II. The important point is that every episode should explore an aspect of the show's setup. If the show is Morph, it should explore one of the aspects of the main character's inner flaw. If the show is Myth, it should be an episode of the myth—for example, a murder-mystery-court-case in an episode of *Law & Order*.

It's a mistake, then, to write an episode that goes off on a tangent and ignores the premise of the series as a whole. And that's why it's important to have at least an idea of what the series' theoretical Act III would be like.

Even though most TV shows never have an Act III, remember how we discussed in the feature context that the Act II is just the route the story takes from Act I to Act III. In television terms, the Act II consists of the episodes. If the writer starts writing episodes without having an Act III in mind, that's the equivalent of a feature writer's striking out on Act II without knowing how the screenplay is going to end.

In *The Sopranos*, for example, Act III can be imagined as one of two possibilities: that Tony will end up either dead because he got too nice, or alone because he got too mean. That gives the writers something to write toward. This is especially important in the case of television because the creator generally doesn't write all the episodes himself, so he has to give the show's writers a roadmap to follow.

◆ ◆ ◆

The next chapter will deal with the TV version of the sequel: the spinoff.

EXERCISE

Screen the pilot and some episodes of *House*. Ask yourself what feature you would write featuring the Evolution of the character, and what feature you would write featuring Failed Evolution.

Then ask yourself how you could slow those features down so they'd take five years of episodes to complete, all the while keeping the audience guessing which ending they were going to see.

CHAPTER THIRTEEN

TELEVISION SPINOFFS

THE CHALLENGE FACING THE PRODUCERS of a TV show who are interested in creating a spinoff series are very similar to those facing the producers of a feature sequel: how can they duplicate the appeal of the original to ensure an audience, while at the same time making it different enough that critics (and viewers) won't say it's the exact same show.

And again the key is the Inner Game. The writer has to come up with a new Inner Game for the spinoff. It's a good idea to make the spinoff's main character and his or her Inner Game distinctive from the original's.

A good example is *CSI: Miami*, a spinoff from *CSI: Crime Scene Investigation*. The danger is obvious — if the shows are too similar, the accusations may come that it's the same show, simply set in a different city. But the producers came up with a way to get a very different product.

How? In the original *CSI*, the main character is Gil Grissom, whose interest week-to-week is in the science — he loves forensics, especially insects and the clues they might provide. This love of science and puzzle-solving pervades the show. Not that the other characters are clones of Grissom, but they tend to share his intellectual orientation toward the job.

CSI: Miami is quite different. Its main character, Horatio Caine, is interested in the morality, the right and wrong, of each case. He's head of the forensics unit, but his interest isn't in solving the puzzle for its own sake, it's in getting the bad guy. Whether he's pulling off his sunglasses or putting his hands on his jutting hips, Caine is at heart a moralist, not a scientist.

And, just as in the original *CSI*, the main character's attitude is echoed by the other characters. Of course, since the spinoff, like the original, is about using forensic science to catch criminals, that intellectual pursuit comes into play, but it's the variation in overall tone that makes the two shows feel so different.

The various *CSI* series are, of course, largely Myth—Sherlock Holmes and Monster. In this respect the shows are quite similar. But a Myth show will get a lot of its tone and flavor from the Morph elements: the main character and his Inner Game. By changing that aspect, you can come up with a comfortably familiar show that feels different enough to pass muster.

Of course, the only people who have to worry about spinoffs are those who have already created successful series, so let me wish that you should have this problem.

◆ ◆ ◆

The next part of the book will deal with the question of whether screenplays can ever succeed without conforming to the Inner Game theory.

EXERCISE

Screen episodes of *Law & Order*, *Law & Order: SVU*, *Law & Order: Criminal Intent*, and *Law & Order: Los Angeles*. Note how the producers changed the format in each spinoff to make for a distinct sequel.

SVU concentrates on a specific slice of the law (sexual offenses), and is also interesting in that it originally concentrated much more on the cops' home lives, although it abandoned that at some point. It also keeps the cops more involved, with less of an abrupt handoff from cops to DAs.

Criminal Intent focuses on open mysteries instead of closed (the audience knows who committed the crime) and concentrates on the rather eccentric interrogations by its quirky main character.

And the latest spinoff, *Law & Order: Los Angeles*, goes back to the original template, hoping that its West Coast locale will give it a distinctive flavor.

Which of the techniques do you think works the best? Can you think of any more spinoff variations that could work?

Part Six TWISTING THE PARADIGM

Up to this point, I've laid out the Inner Game of Screenwriting model—that the Inner Game is the key to writing a compelling screenplay. This raises an interesting question: Is this model the only way to write a successful screenplay? Can the rules be broken and still result in an audience-pleasing script? In a few cases, it can be pulled off.

CHAPTER FOURTEEN

SOMETIMES THE INNER GAME IS IMPLIED

THE EVOLUTION SCREENPLAY is so common, so ingrained in audiences, that even when a film falls short of fulfilling the model, the audience sometimes fills in the blanks.

For example, let's look at *The Proposal*, starring Sandra Bullock. The trailer sets up the story: heartless boss Margaret Tate (Bullock) arranges a marriage of convenience to her long-suffering assistant Andrew Paxton (Ryan Reynolds) so she can avoid being deported. Instantly the audience knows exactly where the story will go: the heartless boss will learn the error of her ways, become a better person, and find that she actually loves the poor guy she's been oppressing.

It's so predictable, it might as well be a Kabuki drama. Most of us could probably skip going to the theater and still give a good enough summary to fool the unwary.

This utter predictability can have two different effects, though: for some it will make a film sound so uninteresting and unsurprising that they'll skip it altogether, but for others, their expectations will be so strong as to survive even if the film fails to completely satisfy them.

In the case of *The Proposal*, I think it fails to conform to its template. Act I doesn't clearly set up Margaret's flaw. She's treated as if she's Meryl Streep's Miranda Priestly from *The Devil Wears Prada*, but she isn't nearly as smart, mean, or three-dimensional.

When Margaret's threatened with deportation (to Canada!), she cooks up a scheme to marry Andrew. She blurts out to their boss that they've secretly gotten engaged and are on their way to Andrew's hometown in Alaska to break the news to his family. Andrew agrees to go along with her charade in return for a promotion to editor.

In Act II, they hang out at his family's mansion (turns out his rich dad pretty much owns the whole town) as her potential in-laws try to get to know her. But instead of dealing with any inner flaw of Margaret's, the second act shows her coping with such horrors as dial-up Internet and unattractive male strippers. So the flaw that wasn't specified in Act I isn't fleshed out in Act II.

We also find out that the assistant's dream of being an editor is opposed by Rich Dad, and that Grandma is a nut who practices some benign sort of prancing-around-a-bonfire witchcraft. In short, Act II concentrates on pretty much everything but whether Margaret is going to overcome her (poorly set up) flaw.

Act III, however, conforms to the Evolution Archetype. Margaret confesses to everyone, including the pursuing U.S. immigration official, that she has conspired to evade federal law through a fraudulent marriage and should be deported back to Canada. But just as she's about to leave, Andrew confesses that he loves her and she realizes that—you guessed it—she loves him too. Somehow they decide to get married and live happily ever after.

My point about this movie is that even with bad Acts I and II, the Act III makes the movie work. Why? I don't think this would succeed in every case, but it works here because the story is so familiar, so well-worn, that it almost doesn't matter what goes on so long as the ending works.

Of course, I wouldn't advise a screenwriter to count on this. I still think this movie would have worked better if the Act I setup were clearer and Act II built on it. But it shows the power of the Inner Game that even when it's only partially developed, it nonetheless can satisfy the audience sufficiently to make a movie successful.

◆ ◆ ◆

The next chapter looks at another case in which a screenplay can succeed without much of an Inner Game.

EXERCISE

Screen *Ransom*, starring Mel Gibson.

In this film, Tom Mullen (Gibson) is a rich businessman whose son is kidnapped by renegade cop Jimmy Shaker (Gary Sinise) and a gang of criminals. At first Mullen is willing to pay a large ransom, but he realizes the kidnappers are likely to kill his son even if he pays, so he instead offers the money to anyone who helps arrest or kill them.

This is the premise, and it's neither a Morph nor a Myth story. Mullen doesn't Evolve, and isn't really trying to kill Shaker—he's trying to get his son back. It's not really a Monster story.

But at the end, Shaker kills his crew and asks for the reward. Mullen is going to give it to him, but realizes he's the kidnapper, and in the last ten minutes of the movie, it turns into a Monster movie. Mullen Kills The Monster, and the movie raked it in ($310 million worldwide on an estimated budget of $80 million) because of the Mythic ending.

Question: How could you change the story so that the Monster Archetype would be more consistently applied?

CHAPTER FIFTEEN

SOMETIMES THE OUTER GAME IS ENOUGH

WHAT IF YOU'RE UNBELIEVABLY GREAT at constructing scenes, writing dialog—all that Outer Game/builder stuff? Can a screenplay or movie have an Outer Game so good that the lack of an Inner Game can be overlooked? Not often, but occasionally.

Case in point, the Coen Brothers' first movie, *Blood Simple*. It's a complicated story of jealousy and murder, with most of the characters ending up dead. No one particularly Evolves or Devolves, and there's no Monster or other Myth story. The ride, in Inner Game terms, doesn't go anywhere.

But it's so much fun along the way.

The scenes are surprising, the dialog crackles. The cinematography is great. By the time you get to the end and realize it all doesn't add up to much, you can't take back the great time you've enjoyed.

This is true of much of the Coen Brothers' work, including *Fargo*, which won them an Oscar for their original screenplay. Why did it win? Well, nowadays there's a substantial group of influential people who agree with film critic Roger Ebert, who wrote that "Films like *Fargo* are why I love the movies."

The truth is, artists in many fields have eventually come to believe that their craft is more important than any underlying objective. Take painting, for example. Back a couple of hundred years ago, painters depicted people to try to show something about people. Of course the great masters developed technique, but they developed technique in order to better accomplish their goal, which was to show something about the human condition.

But then along came the newer, non-representational schools of painting, like Abstract Expressionism. Those painters, and the critics who loved their work, eschewed trying to show viewers anything about people. Instead, they simply painted, putting colors on canvas. Critics supported their work, coming up with theories such as that painters were trying to prove the flatness of the canvas, but I'm not sure who exactly was on the other side of that argument.

A similar phenomenon has occurred in fiction writing. Shakespeare wrote some of the greatest, most memorable lines in the history of the English language, but he didn't do it to show off how flowery he could be. He did it to serve his stories, his themes, to more clearly express what he wanted to express, which again were his observations about the human condition.

And for a long time, most writers did the same. They worked on their language to further their goal, which was to better tell their stories. But more recently there's a group of novelists who seem to think that their goal is not to tell a story so much as to show off their writing. B.R. Myers wrote a famous article and book attacking modern writers for striving to use "the greatest number of standout sentences, regardless of whether or not they fit the context."

As blogger Walter Russell Mead puts it:

> Almost everywhere one looks in American intellectual institutions there is a hypertrophy of the theoretical, galloping credentialism and a withering of the real. In literature, critics and theoreticians erect increasingly complex structures of interpretation and reflection—while the general audience for good literature diminishes from year to year. We are moving towards a society in which a tiny but very well credentialed minority obsessively produces arcane and self-referential (but carefully peer reviewed) theory about texts that nobody reads.

It would appear that screenwriting has reached the same point as these other arts. The original idea of screenwriting and filmmaking was to evoke in the audience an emotional experience, and innovations were useful precisely to the extent that they furthered that goal. But today we've reached the point at which some viewers, and especially some critics, are so tired of conventional, storytelling movies that they'll go wild for films that avoid a coherent or rewarding narrative. Fortunately, the high cost of making a movie, compared to publishing a book, means that pleasing the audience is still important.

So if you're old-fashioned enough to still be trying to consistently satisfy audiences, stick with the Inner Game. Unless you are—like the Coens—so brilliant at Outer Game that you can succeed as they have.

◆ ◆ ◆

In the next chapter, we'll see if a screenplay can succeed while deliberately denying the value of the Inner Game.

EXERCISE

This can be true with a television series more easily than with features. After all, if you've enjoyed a TV show for several years, it's easy to ignore the ultimate failure of the show's overall Inner Game.

Screen *Lost*'s pilot and final episode. The pilot sets up the series as Sherlock Holmes—what is this crazy island? Does the final episode pay off that Myth Archetype? How could you change the final episode so it did? Or how could you change the setup so the final episode ended the Archetype in a more satisfying way?

CHAPTER SIXTEEN

SUBVERTING THE MODEL

THIS BOOK HAS LAID OUT THE THEORY that the Inner
Game—most often one of positive Evolution of the main
character—is the key to making a screenplay work. Which
raises the question: Can a screenwriter succeed while deliberately
flouting this model? By writing a screenplay that calls the whole
conventional enterprise into question?

Answer: Occasionally. *Very* occasionally.

Case in point—*Unforgiven*. A revival of the Western,
Unforgiven stars Clint Eastwood as William Munny, a murderous
gunslinger who gave up that life for his wife, who has since passed
away, leaving him a farmer with a young son.

So, at the outset, Munny is kind of good—an honest farmer,
no longer a killer—but he's also kind of bad, because we sense he's
faking it, frustrated in his new life, uncomfortable with himself.
To repeat—at the beginning of the film, he's neither bad, and
thus ripe for Evolution, nor good, ready for a Staying The Course

or Devolution story. He's somewhere in between. Doesn't look too promising, at least from the Inner Game of Screenwriting point of view.

Munny gets called on by a kid who tells him he's heard of a bounty being offered on a man who cut up a prostitute. He wants to team up with Munny to kill the guy and claim the reward. Munny refuses to go with him, but then reconsiders and rides off to visit his old friend and partner Ned Logan (Morgan Freeman) and enlist him in the scheme. Then the two of them ride after the kid to join up with him.

Standing in their way is Little Bill Daggett (Gene Hackman), the sheriff of the town where the woman was hurt and an amoral former gunslinger himself. Daggett does not want people riding into his town to collect the reward, and he stands ready to beat and, if necessary, kill anyone who tries.

After Ned Logan is brutally murdered as a warning, Munny reconnects with the gunslinger within, leaving Daggett and a bunch of other bad guys in his bloody wake. The movie ends with Munny returning to his farm to resume his quiet life. He is a little worse off—he has blood on his hands again—but also a little better off—he seems more comfortable with himself than he seemed at the outset.

It is often said that *Unforgiven* deconstructs the western film. It plays with its conventions, turning them on their heads. What separates good guys and bad guys, what differentiates good violence from bad violence—the way these questions are answered in the typical western are continually challenged. Even in the little things, as when Eastwood tries to use a liquor bottle in a fight but is instead beaten to the ground, the screenplay points out how westerns work and how fantasy-based they are when you really take a close look.

So it's no great leap to interpret the overall story as also deliberately challenging the Inner Game convention that the main character should undergo a significant change. The movie seems to be saying that that's no more true than any of the western conventions it has upended, that it's okay to tell a story in which no one changes significantly, either for the better or for the worse. It eschews Inner Game—not accidentally, but deliberately.

EXERCISE

Again, this can work well in television series.

Screen the pilot and final episode of *The Sopranos*. Through the run of the show, Tony Soprano alternately progresses and regresses in his quest to Evolve. But in the controversial final episode, the screen goes black, giving the audience the message that the show is leaving Tony in the state in which it found him, without coming to a conclusion as to whether he will ultimately overcome his flaw or succumb to it. This ending was quite controversial— some viewers loved it, and others hated it. How could the writer have ended the story in a more conventional way? Think of an Evolution ending and a Devolution ending. Did the writer pick the best way to wrap up the series?

Part Seven
X-RAY THAT
SCREENPLAY

In this final part, you'll learn how to look at a screenplay and evaluate its Inner Game by doing what I call a **Screenplay X-Ray**.

CHAPTER SEVENTEEN

DOING A SCREENPLAY X-RAY

FIRST, READ THE ENTIRE SCREENPLAY. And do this without a pencil! You're not marking your favorite scenes or lines, you're looking at the script as a whole to see if the Inner Game works. So no notes and no folding over page corners.

STEP ONE: IS THERE A MORPH ELEMENT TO THE SCREENPLAY?

When you're done reading the entire script, ask yourself: From beginning to end, does it mainly tell the story of a character's change? Usually this will be the main character, but in rare cases it's another. Since Evolution is the most common variation, ask yourself: Does the main character Evolve or grow into a healthier, happier version by the end of the screenplay? If so, you're dealing with a Morph screenplay, Evolution type.

If the character clearly changes for the worse rather than for the better, you have a Devolution story.

If the character remains at the same level—usually healthy—but in the course of the Outer Game has to resist and reject temptations, multiple times, then you have a Staying The Course story.

Finally, if the character's psychological/emotional health moves up then down, or down then up, then you have one of those Inner Games with an unusual shape, like the Redemption of *An Education*.

The big thing is, of course, that the screenplay has to have some sort of Inner Game. If there's no Morph Inner Game, move on to the next step and hope.

STEP TWO: IS THERE A MYTH ELEMENT TO THE SCREENPLAY?

Does the story largely consist of trying to kill a monster, whether natural, supernatural, human, or institutional? To destroy it or bring it down? Then you're probably dealing with a Monster story.

Does it feature a character who starts the screenplay or movie as humble and infantilized but ends the story not so much changed as revealed as a powerful, brilliant adult? Then you're dealing with a Cinderella story.

Is the story a detective story, either with real detectives or other characters who are acting in that role, in which the driving narrative is the quest to solve a mystery? Will that story be successfully completed when the mystery is solved and understood? Then you've got a Sherlock Holmes story. And remember that Sherlock Holmes will often transition to Monster, especially when first solving a crime, then catching and punishing the criminal.

Does the main character travel to a totally unfamiliar world, where he encounters incredible obstacles as he strives to get back to his normal environment? See if it works as Oz.

Does a character start out as metaphorically dead, due to a complete lack of love in his or her life? Is he or she awakened from that state when another professes love? You may have a Sleeping Beauty story.

Remember that the Morph and Myth categories are not mutually exclusive: a screenplay can have both types, resulting in a hybrid. Take, for example, *Avatar*.

This film is definitely a hybrid. Director/screenwriter James Cameron threw a lot of Inner Game into his 3D epic. First, the main character, Jake Sully, undergoes a profound Evolution. A former marine, he starts the movie quite damaged, having lost the use of his legs and, more importantly, his brother. When he joins the expedition to Pandora, the other soldiers there do not welcome him, perhaps seeing in him a dangerous future they do not want to acknowledge. Everything combined has left Jake isolated and embittered.

By the end of the film, Jake has been transformed. He has become a Na'vi, a fully-accepted member of Pandora's native tribe. And he has mated for life with Neytiri, the Na'vi female who has taught him the way of the tribe. He is no longer alone. The Evolution in Jake's character is obvious.

On the Myth side, there is a clear Monster story. The monsters? The humans, as especially embodied by the ruthless, apparently unbeatable Colonel Quaritch.

Jake leads the Na'vi against the human military forces, and the Na'vi are eventually victorious. His mate Neytiri kills Colonel Quaritch, and the surviving humans are forced to leave Pandora.

In addition, Jake's Evolution story is so extreme it becomes Myth, a Cinderella story. Remember, the first time we see Jake he can't walk, a symbol of a childlike state. This is repeated when he first tries to walk in the avatar body—he is uncertain and stumbling.

Later, as he tries to learn the ways of the Na'vi in his avatar body, he again has great difficulty keeping up with the Neytiri. But he slowly improves.

By the end of the film, Jake's transformation goes well beyond Evolution, well beyond becoming healthier or overcoming a flaw. He has become a member of a group, but he is no ordinary member. He has become one of their greatest heroes and has saved them from exile, and perhaps extinction. He has tamed the beast and killed the monster. He has married the princess and become their king. He has Come of Age.

IF THE SCREENPLAY YOU'RE READING HAS NEITHER A MORPH INNER GAME NOR A MYTH ONE, IT IS UNLIKELY TO SUCCEED.

This is in keeping with the theory of this book. Many screenplays, even the produced ones, fail because they simply lack either a Morph or a Myth Inner Game. If that's the case, you have to go back to designing your screenplay and come up with an Inner Game, whether Morph or Myth, that will drive it. Without one, the screenplay probably won't work.

STEP THREE: IF YOUR SCREENPLAY HAS A MORPH INNER GAME, DOES THE ACT II STAY ON THAT STORY?

If you've found you're dealing with a Morph Inner Game, turn your attention to the middle of the screenplay. Does it stay on the story or does it go off on irrelevant (to the Inner Game) tangents, maybe for the sake of comedy bits or action sequences? To really work, a screenplay's middle has to stay on the Inner Game path set up by the beginning and end.

If your screenplay is Myth, there's less of a potential problem that the middle will stray from the path set out from beginning to end. If a character is trying to kill a Monster, he's probably not going to stop to play some golf in Act II.

But the Myth screenplay has another potential problem:

STEP FOUR: IF YOUR SCREENPLAY IS MYTH, DOES THE OUTER GAME WORK SYMBOLICALLY AS AN INNER GAME?

The most common form of Myth story is Monster. Remember how it's supposed to work: the monster in the story, whether creature, human, or institution, symbolizes a human flaw. Killing it symbolizes overcoming the flaw. So it's very important to look at the story and see if it works in this regard.

The analogue to an Evolution story would be to fight the monster, winning a little and losing a lot, until, in the end, the monster is killed. That would be symbolically equivalent to the main character fighting his inner flaw and eventually Evolving by defeating it.

Another possibility would be for the monster to eventually win. That would be analogous to a Devolution story in which the main character succumbs to his inner flaw.

The thing to avoid is writing a Monster story that *doesn't* translate into a Morph story. A story, for example, in which characters flee from a monster which then, for reasons having nothing to do with the characters, disappears on its own, doesn't work symbolically. You can't overcome your inner flaw by running away from it. Although if you run from your flaw and it kills you, you may have a successful Run Away! story.

If you have a Myth story, but it doesn't quite work, you have to go back and change it so it does.

In summary, what you're doing when performing a Screenplay X-Ray is asking two questions:

1. Is there an Inner Game, either Morph or Myth?

2. If there is an Inner Game, is it well-constructed?

If the answer to these two questions is yes, your screenplay can be successful. If the answer to either is no, you've got a problem and some rewriting to do.

Let's illustrate the Screenplay X-Ray process by doing an X-Ray on a recent movie, *Unknown*, starring Liam Neeson. This will contain spoilers, so if you haven't seen the movie and don't want to know what happens, you've been warned.

The main element at the beginning of the film is, obviously, the Myth Archetype of Sherlock Holmes. A mystery is presented in Act I—Neeson's character Dr. Martin Harris goes to Berlin with his wife for a professional conference, then is in an auto accident and spends four days in a coma. When he wakes up, his wife hasn't been looking for him, and when he goes to see her, she acts like she doesn't recognize him and there's a man who's taken his place, both as her husband and as Dr. Martin Harris. Harris's goal is to solve this mystery and find out what's happened.

It's a little unusual as a Sherlock Holmes story, because it's not solving a crime, but it's pretty interesting. Is it solved in Act III? Actually, it's solved earlier than that, toward the end of Act II.

This means that this Archetype won't be able to carry the film through to its end, and that presents a screenwriting challenge.

Does this mystery story stay on track as the movie progresses? After he's almost murdered, Harris seeks help from an ex-East German secret policeman, who goes off and does some research to figure everything out. This is not terribly satisfying dramatically, since he does this without Harris's involvement.

It's interesting to note that *Unknown* was adapted from a novel, and the East German's side story may have been interesting in a book, where we could hear his thoughts and learn more about his history. But in the film, watching him type on a computer and open mail is pretty dull. In fact he's the one who ends up solving the mystery first, after which he commits suicide without telling Harris what he's discovered.

And when Harris does finally figure out what's been happening, it's because the bad guy tells him the answer while getting ready to kill him. It's like when Batman's supervillains would taunt him, giving him the chance to overcome them and escape.

Anyway, the solution to the mystery is that Harris isn't really Harris at all—he's really an unnamed member of an international assassination team, and "Dr. Martin Harris" is a cover identity he's concocted for his assignment in Berlin. As a result of his traumatic auto accident, he got confused and believed he was this fictional person.

Since this mystery is solved so early, the Sherlock Holmes story is over and it's not clear where the screenplay should go from that point. To keep the movie going, the screenwriters have to start up a whole new Inner Game. Actually, they start up two—one Morph, the other Myth.

The Morph Archetype is a version of Revival. When the audience finds out Harris isn't the nice doctor he's appeared to be, but is instead an assassin, it has the effect of an Apparent Devolution. He's gone from good guy to bad, at least as far as we can see. When he laments finding out he's really a killer, another character says that what matters is what happens now, a clear call for him to re-Evolve back to good guy in what's left of the film. Revival.

This Morph story unfortunately has some problems. On the one hand, we don't see Harris doing anything really bad, like killing someone; we just see him preparing for the job he came to Berlin for. So his Apparent Devolution isn't terribly convincing. On the other hand, it's not at all clear why he should Evolve — he's confused because of a head injury, but clearly he thought being an assassin was okay before he got hurt, so why shouldn't we assume he'll be comfortable with it again once he's fully recovered?

To facilitate his Revival, the script introduces a Monster story about stopping what's left of the assassination team from completing their deadly assignment. But this is a rather weak Monster story: the team isn't killing people wholesale or generally wreaking havoc; they're working to kill one character we don't really know, we've never seen either of the two remaining assassins kill anyone, so they're not terribly Monstrous, and one of them was initially introduced to us as Harris's loving wife, so we kind of like her.

In the end, Harris does stop the assassination. Then he and the beautiful illegal immigrant cab driver who saved him from drowning in his accident go off with new passports, presumably unfindable by the bad guys. But they're not a couple, or haven't been set up as such, so they're just…running away. As the last scene in the film, it doesn't end any of the Inner Game stories.

So both the Archetypes introduced in Act III are not very involving or satisfying. Whether this film will ultimately succeed will depend on whether audiences' enjoyment of the initial Sherlock Holmes story outweighs their disappointment in the late-coming Revival and Monster stories.

EXERCISE

Screen several successful movies and do full-scale Screenplay X-Rays on them.

Then do one on an unsuccessful movie.

Do the X-Rays explain the audiences' different reactions?

CHAPTER EIGHTEEN

SUMMARY

S O WHAT HAVE WE LEARNED FROM THIS BOOK?

First, the big meta-point is that audiences are looking—not necessarily consciously, of course—for a particular thing when they watch a movie: they're looking for Inner Game. While **Outer Game** is the exterior story—the main character is trying to win the chess championship, or steal a priceless coin collection from an impenetrable bank—**Inner Game** is what's going on, emotionally and psychologically, inside the characters.

If you have a good Inner Game, audiences will likely spark to your screenplay; if you don't have a good Inner Game, they're unlikely to do so.

Next, what exactly is Inner Game? It's most often the main character overcoming an inner flaw, and in doing so becoming a better person. When we see, onscreen, the main character doing this, it's the most common sort of Inner Game: Evolution. The character starts out flawed, and—as a result of going through the Outer Game—is forced to confront and overcome this flaw. How this relates to the Outer Game varies—sometimes the character has to overcome his inner flaw to achieve the Outer Game's goal; other times she has to renounce the Outer Game goal in order to overcome her inner flaw. The Outer Game is simply the screenplay's device to force or facilitate the Inner Game, the character's inner change.

Next we learned that there are two distinct sorts of Inner Game. The ones we were just talking about, in which the audience sees a character make a change, are called **Morph Archetypes**. But there's another, quite different, group in which characters change *symbolically*, rather than literally, called **Myth Archetypes**.

Starting with Morph, we went through the various types of Morph Inner Game Archetypes.

Evolution is the most common. It's the one in which the character overcomes an inner flaw to become a better person (*The Queen*). But there are others.

Devolution, in which the character starts out relatively unflawed, but succumbs to an inner flaw, becoming a worse person in the process (*The Godfather*). Less common than Evolution, but potentially very effective.

And **Staying The Course**, in which the character starts unflawed and stays that way, refusing to succumb to an inner flaw (*300*).

Then there are several additional **Morph Archetypes** that combine those basic three:

Unsuccessful Evolution, in which the character starts flawed, begins to Evolve, but then Devolves back, ending up as bad as or even worse than he started (*The Wrestler*).

Fall & Revival, in which the character first Devolves and then Evolves back to her original state (*An Education*).

Staying The Course with an Evolution Pop, in which the character successfully Stays the Course and, at the very end,

Evolves a little to become an even better person (*The Dark Knight*).

And **Evolve & Maintain**, in which the character Evolves quickly, but then must resist strong temptations to Devolve back to his starting point (*The Verdict*).

Finally, on the Morph front, we noted that because character change is measured from the audience's point of view, there can be **Apparent Evolution** or **Apparent Devolution**, even if the characters don't actually Evolve or Devolve. This is the result of the character's concealing his true nature from the other characters—and the audience—so when he reveals that he's better (*Eastern Promises*) or worse (*Training Day*) than he at first appears, the audience gets the appearance and emotional effect of Evolution or Devolution.

Apparent Evolution can also occur as a result of the screenwriter's warping of the time sequence, for example starting the movie at a character's low point and ending at a high point to give the appearance of Evolution, even though those points are not actually the first and last points in the screenplay's timeline (*Pulp Fiction*).

Then we looked at using the **Enneagram**, a popular psychological tool, to build consistent and meaningful Morph Archetypes. The Enneagram divides people into nine types and describes them in great detail. It also describes healthier and less healthy versions of each type. A screenwriter seeking to show a character overcoming an inner flaw can simply start the character at a less healthy version of his Enneagram type and let him change to a healthier version. It's a great tool for screenwriting.

Then we moved to the Myth Archetypes, which work symbolically. First, and most common, is **Monster,** in which the character defeats a monster of some sort—whether a literal monster, an alien, an evil human, a disease, or something else threatening and ongoing. In a Monster screenplay, the character need not change for the better, because his killing of the monster is itself a *symbol* of overcoming an inner flaw (*Jaws*).

There are notable variations on Monster.

Run Away! is a form that often doesn't work. When the character doesn't fight with the monster, but instead just runs away, it's symbolically unsatisfying if at the end of the screenplay the monster dies for reasons that have nothing to do with the character (*War of the Worlds*). You can't overcome an inner flaw by running away.

But Run Away! can work if, in the end, the protaganist is **Killed By The Monster** (*The Blair Witch Project*). Just as Monster is symbolically analogous to the Morph Archetype of Evolution, Run Away! and losing to the monster is symbolically analogous to the Morph Archetype of Devolution.

Nice Monster, in which the monster turns out to be far better than the humans trying to kill it, is a variation that can confuse the audience (*King Kong*). How can your inner flaw not be a bad thing?

Wrong Monster, in which the character is tricked into killing someone other than the real monster, which remains a threat, and as a result faces a forbidding future rather than a hopeful one (*Basic Instinct*).

And **Sherlock Holmes,** in which a mystery is the monster being killed. Mysteries are threatening because they make us doubt that reason can deal with reality. By solving the mystery, the detective reasserts the primacy of reason over chaos.

Then there are the Myth Archetypes that symbolically represent stories other than Evolution or Devolution.

Cinderella represents growing from child to adult. The character starts the story out child-like, oppressed by parental figures and favored siblings, then progresses and stands revealed at the end as a strong, competent adult (*The Bourne Identity*).

Oz has the character going to a completely unfamiliar land, where he deals with extremely demanding challenges while trying to get back to his original world (*The Wizard of Oz*). This Archetype symbolically represents the common—incorrect—hope and belief that an external change is all we need to make our lives idyllic.

In **Sleeping Beauty** stories, the character starts the story meta-phorically dead and is brought back to life by another's expression of love (*Casablanca*). The symbolic meaning of this Archetype is that a life without love isn't life at all, and that someone living such a life needs to be rescued from it by finding love.

Realization is a non-Archetype that is sometimes tried but doesn't work (*In the Valley of Elah*) and should be avoided. A character doesn't really overcome a flaw, rather he "realizes something," generally a political idea the screenwriter thinks is very important. But because the character doesn't actually Evolve, either literally or symbolically, these stories don't involve the audience.

We looked at what is commonly considered an Archetype but is not—**Quest**. A character's Quest is an Archetype only if it fits into one of the specific Myth categories: if a character's Quest is to kill a monster, it's a Monster story. If a character finds himself in a strange, new world and his Quest is to overcome problems and get back to his old world, it could be an Oz story. But if his Quest is to walk across post-Apocalyptic America to California while carrying the world's only remaining copy of the Bible to deliver it to a group that will print it and respread the word of God (*The Book of Eli*), that's not a Myth Archetype at all. It's an Outer Game in need of a Morph Inner Game.

Next we discussed weaving the Inner and Outer Games into a satisfying screenplay. In the Morph category, a screenplay must introduce the character flaw in Act I, pay off the Evolution or Devolution in Act III, and—very important—stick to that character change throughout Act II. Many screenplays go wrong by getting off the Inner Game in Act II.

In the Myth category, the important thing is to make sure the Outer Game is symbolically satisfying.

In both cases, we introduced a method of graphing the Inner Game and Outer Game, or the Outer Game and Symbolic Meaning, a method that will help screenwriters stay on course as they plot out their scripts.

Then we covered the special situations of adaptations, sequels, and remakes. The bottom line is that these features follow the same rules as any others: their success is determined by the quality of their Inner Games. A screenwriter dealing in this arena has to be just as careful to have an effective Inner Game as she would be if writing any other feature.

Next we moved on to television. The Inner Game theory applies just as well to television as to features, but it applies at the level of TV series. A series must have a coherent Inner Game, whether Morph or Myth, to succeed. Most half-hour series are Morph, but many hour-long series are Myth, including the familiar police procedurals, which combine Sherlock Holmes and Monster.

Then we dealt with the exceptions—feature films that succeed without totally conforming to the Inner Game theory. Some movies succeed by finishing the Inner Game well, even if the setup and development are ineffective (*The Proposal*).

Some succeed because of amazing execution of Outer Game, even though the Inner Game is lacking (*Blood Simple*). And, finally, it's occasionally possible to attract audiences to a movie that denies the Inner Game altogether, that says it's all right to have a movie in which no one changes either for the better or for the worse (*Unforgiven*).

Last, we learned to perform a **Screenplay X-Ray** to evaluate a screenplay's or movie's Inner Game. The Screenplay X-Ray will help someone evaluate either a produced movie or a screenplay in progress to see what's there and what work is yet to be done.

CHAPTER NINETEEN

WHERE TO GO FROM HERE

NOW WHAT SHOULD YOU DO?

Remember the premise of this book:

■ **A relentless focus on the Inner Game is what you need to make your screenplay succeed.**

Apply it as you write your scripts. Make sure you formulate and use compelling Inner Games in every screenplay you write.

The other thing you should do is continue your screenwriting education, in light of what you've learned here. To go back to the first metaphor of the book, now that you've learned that in golf you're trying to get the ball into the hole in the fewest strokes possible, the advice to keep your head down is going to make more sense. Most of the books, DVDs and courses available have something that can help you be a better writer, and now you'll be better equipped to evaluate them and take from them what works for you.

For example, when a book tells you that you absolutely need an opponent for your main character, ask yourself why that would be true. If the opponent is essential to the main character's Evolution, then okay. But if it's not, question the conventional wisdom. Maybe we mainly need opponents so the Outer Games don't end too quickly—after all, if a guy's trying to deliver drugs to another guy in Detroit, it'll all be over pretty quickly unless someone is trying to stop him. On the other hand, if you're writing *Juno*, she's going to be pregnant for nine months whether there's an opponent or not, so maybe you don't need one.

The meta-point of this book is that screenwriters need a theory. You absolutely shouldn't start typing without some notion of what you're trying to give the audience. That's what this book does, give you a theory: Audiences crave the Inner Game.

Watch movies and get used to watching your own reactions as you do. What are you enjoying about the movie? What are you hating? When are you interested, and when are you bored? If you can figure out what you like, you're on the way to figuring out what an audience will like. Don't be a screenwriter's screenwriter; be an audience's screenwriter.

That's why I came up with the Inner Game of Screenwriting, and I sincerely hope it works for you.

Good luck!

ABOUT THE AUTHOR

 SANDY FRANK left an elite Wall Street law firm to be a writer for *Late Night with David Letterman*. He worked on that show for four years, sharing in four Emmy Awards and creating the Velcro Suit.

Moving to Los Angeles, Sandy worked on shows ranging from sketch (*In Living Color*) to sitcom (*The Jamie Foxx Show*) to drama (*Mister Sterling*). He also did rewrite work on a number of feature screenplays.

Analytical by nature, the former math major and computer programmer has at each stage of his writing career aimed to dissect how various formats work. This effort has come together in *The Inner Game of Screenwriting*. Now every screenwriter can share in that knowledge.

Sandy Frank lives in Calabasas, California.

For information about script consultation services, please contact Sandy at *sandy@innerscreenwriting.com*.

{ THE MYTH OF MWP }

In a dark time, a light bringer came along, leading the curious and the frustrated to clarity and empowerment. It took the well-guarded secrets out of the hands of the few and made them available to all. It spread a spirit of openness and creative freedom, and built a storehouse of knowledge dedicated to the betterment of the arts.

The essence of the Michael Wiese Productions (MWP) is empowering people who have the burning desire to express themselves creatively. We help them realize their dreams by putting the tools in their hands. We demystify the sometimes secretive worlds of screenwriting, directing, acting, producing, film financing, and other media crafts.

By doing so, we hope to bring forth a realization of 'conscious media' which we define as being positively charged, emphasizing hope and affirming positive values like trust, cooperation, self-empowerment, freedom, and love. Grounded in the deep roots of myth, it aims to be healing both for those who make the art and those who encounter it. It hopes to be transformative for people, opening doors to new possibilities and pulling back veils to reveal hidden worlds.

MWP has built a storehouse of knowledge unequaled in the world, for no other publisher has so many titles on the media arts. Please visit www.mwp.com where you will find many free resources and a 25% discount on our books. Sign up and become part of the wider creative community!

Onward and upward,

Michael Wiese
Publisher/Filmmaker